INSPIRE / PLAN / DISCOVER / EXPERIENCE

BARCELONA
AND CATALONIA

DK EYEWITNESS

BARCELONA
AND CATALONIA

CONTENTS

DISCOVER 6

EXPERIENCE 64

NEED TO KNOW 202

Left: Effervescent colour in Palau de la Música Catalana
Previous page: Catedral de Barcelona lit against the dusky sky
Cover: Park Güell at twilight

DISCOVER

The Barcelona cityscape cut by leafy La Rambla

WELCOME TO BARCELONA AND CATALONIA

Rugged Catalonia and its avant-garde capital are tantalizingly different from the rest of Spain. Here Gaudí's buildings inspire modern-day fairy tales, beaches bite the coast and giants chase through the streets during exuberant festivals. Whatever your dream trip to Barcelona and Catalonia includes, this DK Eyewitness Travel Guide is the perfect companion.

1 Ricardo Bofill's splendid Walden 7 housing project.

2 A sunny day at a packed Costa Brava beach.

3 Tasty street food displayed at La Boqueria.

4 Buzzy café-lined, palm-shaded Plaça Reial.

Tucked in an untamed crook between Pyrenean peaks and the Mediterranean Sea, Catalonia's stunning landscapes brim with natural splendour. Endless sandy beaches and turquoise coves stretch from the wild Costa Brava down into the long, pale strands of the sun-baked Costa Daurada. The snowcapped Pyrenees towers to the north, ideal for alpine sports, while across the heartland vineyards drop in corduroyed terraces. These glorious landscapes, immortalized in the works of Joan Miró and Salvador Dalí, gaze back at us from Catalonia's myriad museums and galleries.

Just as enticing are the region's bustling cities and dreamy medieval villages. Barcelona, the Catalan capital, has inspired artists for centuries. Its spirit is embodied in Picasso's paint, Gaudí's bricks and, more recently, on plates. Barcelona has a stellar foodie reputation, with experimental chefs reinventing classic cuisine and fantastic street food. Other centres are no less alluring. Girona enchants with its beautifully preserved medieval core, while Tarragona has some of the finest Roman monuments in Spain. Skimming the coast, fishing villages offer nonpareil spots to sample freshly grilled sardines with a chilled glass of cava and gorgeous sea views.

So, where to start? We've broken Catalonia down into easily navigable chapters, with detailed itineraries, expert local knowledge and colourful comprehensive maps to help you plan the perfect visit. However long you stay, this Eyewitness guide will ensure that you see the very best that Barcelona and Catalonia have to offer. *Benvingut!* Enjoy the book, and enjoy Barcelona and Catalonia.

REASONS TO LOVE
BARCELONA
AND CATALONIA

Blending Gothic churches with dizzying skyscrapers, traditional parades with a dynamic arts scene, centuries-old taverns with ritzy cocktail bars, Catalonia is a constant contradiction that keeps us coming back for more.

1 GAUDÍ'S BARCELONA

Spain's most famous architect has left his indelible mark across Catalonia's capital, with colourfully scaly rooftops, confection-like façades, intriguing chimneypots and the dazzling spires of the truly iconic Sagrada Família *(p106)*.

WORLD-CLASS ART *2*

Home to abundant museums and galleries, Catalonia lives and breathes art. Seek out the enchanting Dalí Triangle *(p187)* and the canvases of Catalonia's revered masters.

3 FESTIVALS

From cutting-edge electronica to honey and herbs, just about everything is celebrated in style with its own festival. *Festas* break out across the region all year long, but don't miss Barcelona's big one – La Mercè – in September *(p56)*.

MEANDERING AROUND MARKETS 4

Barcelona's La Boqueria tantalizes with its colourful produce and the scent of fresh pastries, but lively markets – fabulous for people-watching – are found in every village.

THE COSTA BRAVA 5

Peppered with stunning little coves chipped out of the shoreline and soaring, chalky cliffs, the Costa Brava offers 60 km (37 miles) of rugged beauty and mellow living.

SITGES'S VIBRANT NIGHTLIFE 6

When night falls, Sitges's (p197) bars and restaurants spill outside. Head to Organic Club, one of Spain's oldest LGBT+ clubs, around 3am, when things really get pumping.

GIRONA *7*

This stunning medieval city, all cobbles and stone arches, was used as a backdrop in *Game of Thrones*. Climb the cathedral steps to see the show's Braavos in real life, then wend through the old-world Jewish Quarter.

8 INNOVATIVE CUISINE

Now mostly retired, Ferran Adrià changed the face of dining around the world with his adventures in molecular gastronomy. Across Catalonia, his protégés showcase his techniques at their own dazzling restaurants.

LA RAMBLA *9*

A mile-long avenue of historic buildings cutting through the heart of old Barcelona, café-lined La Rambla bubbles with life. There's no better place to join locals in the Spanish ritual of the *paseo* (stroll) in the shade of the leafy plane trees.

10 PENEDÈS'S CAVA

Catalonia is the home of cava and tiny Penedès *(p194)* is paradise for aficionados of fizz. Its vineyards are the perfect place to go for tastings and to meet master winemakers.

FC BARÇA 11

Barcelona's most famous football club is "more than a club" for its devout following. Catch the team in action and discover its epic sporting history at Camp Nou *(p146)*.

HUMAN CASTLES 12

A mainstay of Catalan folk culture, these extraordinary human pyramids are both nail-biting and heartwarming, as small children scamper up to the top to add a final few inches and onlookers cheer their support.

EXPLORE
BARCELONA
AND CATALONIA

This guide divides Barcelona into three colour-coded sightseeing areas, as shown on this map. Find out more about each area on the following pages. For sights beyond the city centre see p142, and for Catalonia see p164.

PLAÇA D'ESPANYA

GRAN VIA DE LES CORTS CATALANES

GRAN VIA DE LES CORTS CATALANES

SANT ANTONI

CaxiaForum

Museu Nacional d'Art de Catalunya (MNAC)

EL POBLE SEC

AVINGUDA DEL PARAL·LEL

MONTJUÏC
p124

Museu Olímpic i de l'Esport

Fundació Joan Miró

Estadi Olímpic de Montjuïc

MONTJUÏC

Parc de Montjuïc

Castell de Montjuïc

RONDA DEL LITORAL

SPAIN

Atlantic Ocean

FRANCE

Bilbao · Santander

PORTUGAL

SPAIN

BARCELONA

Madrid · Valencia ·

· Seville

Mediterranean Sea

TRAVESSERA DE GRACIA

GRÀCIA

AVINGUDA DE GAUDÍ

AVINGUDA DIAGONAL

PASSEIG DE SANT JOAN

RAMBLA DE CATALUNYA

PASSEIG DE GRÀCIA

Sagrada
Família

EIXAMPLE

Casa Batlló

EIXAMPLE
p102

PLAÇA DE
LES GLÒRIES
CATALANES

GRAN VIA DE LES CORTS CATALANES

AVINGUDA MERIDIANA

RONDA DE SANT PERE

PLAÇA DE
CATALUNYA

Museu d'Art
Contemporani
(MACBA)

LA RAMBLA

BARRI
GÒTIC

Catedral de
Barcelona

EL RAVAL

Museu
Picasso

OLD TOWN
p66

EL POBLENOU

LA RAMBLA

PLAÇA
REIAL

El Born
Centre

Palau Güell

LA RIBERA

*Parc de la
Ciutadella*

Museu Marítim
and Drassanes

PLAÇA
D'ANTONI
LÓPEZ

Estació
de França

PLAÇA DEL
PORTAL
DE LA PAU

PORT VELL

*Dàrsena
Nacional*

Marina
Port Vell

*Parc de la
Barceloneta*

PORT
OLÍMPIC

BARCELONETA

*Platja
Barceloneta*

*Platja
Sant Sebastià*

*Mediterranean
Sea*

0 metres   500
0 yards   500

N

GETTING TO KNOW
BARCELONA
AND CATALONIA

Buzzing Barcelona and the sun-drenched Costa Brava are big draws, but Catalonia's dreamy Romanesque villages, vineyard-strewn hills, pristine wilderness and soaring mountain landscape are not to be missed. With everything in easy distance, this Spanish region is the perfect destination for city-goers and outdoor enthusiasts alike.

OLD TOWN

PAGE 66

Barcelona's medieval core is a maze of crooked streets and narrow lanes that open dramatically into splendid squares. It's the perfect place to saunter along hairpin alleys, hunt for vintage treasures or just to savour a coffee on a street-side table. Crowned by an enormous Gothic cathedral, the Old Town is home to some of the city's best-loved sights, including the tree-shaded promenade of La Rambla. Lined with a host of enticing shops, charming cafés and tiny tapas bars, and thronging with locals, tourists and performance artists, this far-reaching street is the city's beating heart.

Best for
Medieval buildings and quirky museums

Home to
Catedral de Barcelona, La Rambla, Palau Güell, Palau de la Música Catalana, Museu Picasso

Experience
Sampling tapas in a hidden corner of Barri Gòtic

EIXAMPLE

Laid out in the late 19th century, after the medieval walls were finally dismantled, Eixample is an elegant grid of broad avenues lined with graceful mansions that link the old city to the former villages of Gràcia and Sants. Prosperity and creativity created a perfect storm as the area became a canvas for Modernista architects, with Gaudí's masterpiece – the Sagrada Família – at the centre of it all. Nicknamed "Gaixample", the area is also the heart of Barcelona's lively LGBT+ scene, with specialist bookshops, hip boutiques and chic clubs that pulsate into the early hours.

Best for
Modernisme and LGBT+ life

Home to
Casa Batlló, La Pedrera, Sagrada Família

Experience
A summer jazz concert on the roof of La Pedrera

→

PAGE 124

MONTJUÏC

Rising above the city, Montjuïc has been Barcelona's vantage point for centuries. The journey to the top is a reward in itself, whether strolling through leafy parks, zipping up in the funicular or soaring high in the vertiginous cable car. This tranquil spot, crowned by Castell de Montjuïc, is perfect for a picnic or to take in the Magic Fountain, an extravaganza of colour and music – utterly kitsch and impossible not to love. Yet the museums steal the show. With Catalan treasures, contemporary art and a reproduced Spanish village, Montjuïc is a cultural treasure trove.

Best for
Strolling and picnicking

Home to
Fundació Joan Miró, Museu Nacional d'Art de Catalunya

Experience
Riding the swaying cable car up to the Castell de Montjuïc, admiring the city spread below

PAGE 142

BEYOND THE CENTRE

Before they were absorbed by Barcelona, the hamlets around the city had distinct identities and many retain a small-town atmosphere. Those who venture outside the city centre are rewarded with myriad sights, including the legendary Camp Nou – Europe's biggest football stadium – Gaudí's ginger-bread-like Park Güell and the pretty little Gothic convent at Pedralbes. To escape the heat and crowds, nothing beats hitting the shaded hiking paths that wend up the Collserola hills to Tibidabo and its charmingly old-fashioned funfair.

Best for
Football and fun fairs

Home to
Camp Nou, Monestir de Pedralbes, Park Güell

Experience
Sneaking away from the crowds to the peace and quiet of the Monestir de Pedralbes

CATALONIA

Sun-drenched, pine-fringed beaches nip at the flank of this rugged region, while inland ancient volcanic landscapes give way to the fragrant *matollar* (scrubland) and sloping vineyards. The dazzling Costas Brava and Daurada lure travellers to the coast. Peppered with fishing villages and secret coves, this is *the* place for skewers of freshly grilled sardines and a chilled *cervesa* on the beach. To the north, the alpine playground of the Pyrenees towers above lonely valleys punctuated with Romanesque hamlets. Stepping south, Catalonia is a patchwork of contradictions. Girona is a love letter to a medieval past, while LGBT+-friendly Sitges sizzles with summer shenanigans and a packed programme of festivals. In Tarragona a Roman past collides with seaside fun, and the Dalí Triangle keeps things sublimely surreal.

Best for
Unspoiled coastline and medieval towns

Home to
Monestir de Montserrat, Monestir de Poblet, Girona, Tarragona's Roman ruins, Romanesque Architecture

Experience
Listening to the choir at the Montserrat monastery

←

1 Light fading over majestic Catedral de Barcelona.

2 Standing in the inner courtyard of La Pedrera.

3 Picasso's etchings at El Col·legi d'Arquitectes de Catalunya.

4 A freshly baked spread.

Catalonia is a treasure trove of must-see sights and unique experiences. Covering the length and breadth of the region and taking in vibrant cities and beautiful natural spaces, these itineraries will help you make the most of your trip.

5 HOURS
in Barcelona

Morning

Set out on foot to explore the ever-moody Barri Gòtic *(p98)*, one of the most alluring and best-preserved medieval districts in Europe. First stop on anyone's list should be the magnificent Catedral de Barcelona *(p70)*, dedicated to Santa Eulàlia, one of the city's patron saints, who is buried in an alabaster sarcophagus in the crypt. A lift will carry you up to the rooftop to admire the gargoyles and the stunning views over the ancient city. Back on the ground, wander over to nearby Museu Frederic Marés *(p81)* to enjoy a break in its charming outdoor café. As you cross the enormous Plaça de la Seu, stop outside El Col·legi d'Arquitectes de Catalunya to admire the friezes on the façade created by Norwegian artist Carl Nesjar from drawings made by Picasso, before walking across to the Plaça Catalunya, the city's main hub. From here, amble up boutique-lined Passeig de Gràcia, the wide artery of the elegant Eixample district, laid out in the late 19th century to accommodate horse-drawn carriages of the city's aristocrats. Have your camera at the ready: this neighbourhood is full of picture-perfect Modernista mansions, bakeries and pharmacies, all with hand-painted wooden signs, gorgeous stained-glass, delicate tiles and filigree ironwork.

Afternoon

Stop for a break at El Nacional *(p117)*, where myriad bars and restaurants gather under one gorgeous roof. This former warehouse has been spectacularly renovated to become a stylish gourmet hub and is perfect for lunch. Tuck into tapas and a refreshing glass of cava, then continue your stroll back up the Passeig de Gràcia to admire Gaudí's extraordinary apartment building, La Pedrera *(p114)*, with its swirling, creamy façade. Continue on to reach the famous Illa de la Discòrdia *(p116)*, home to three mansions by the greatest Modernista architects. Casa Lleó i Morera is by Domènech i Montaner, also responsible for the Palau de la Música Catalana *(p76)*, while neighbouring Casa Amatller is by Puig i Cadafalch, who created Casa de les Punxes. The most famous is the colourful Casa Batlló *(p112)*, with its undulating rooftop designed to resemble a scaly dragon's back – unmistakably the work of Antoni Gaudí. Take a tour here to fully appreciate the master's unique imagination inside and out. Finish on a sweet note, with a quick diversion down La Rambla to Escribà *(p86)*, the city's oldest cake shop, brimming with toothsome treats from Día de Muertos-themed cakes to *carquinyolis* (biscotti).

→

1 A lively night out in Gràcia's Carrer de Joan Blanques.

2 Giving thanks on the bronze doors to Sagrada Família.

3 An elaborate handmade cocktail at Paradiso.

4 The dazzling interior of Palau de la Música Catalana.

2 DAYS
in Barcelona

Day 1

Morning Begin with breakfast at the Modernista tavern Els 4 Gats *(p37)*, former haunt of artists including Picasso (who painted the menu). The early Modernista building by Puig i Cadafalch will whet your appetite for a tour of Palau de la Música Catalana *(p76)*, a Modernista masterpiece by Domènech i Montaner. The façade is a riot of colourful mosaics, tiled garlands and sculptures – the enormous inverted skylight of stained glass in the auditorium is breathtaking.

Afternoon Linger over delicious tapas at the tiny Bar del Pla *(p90)* – don't miss the freshly grilled octopus. Later, head to the Museu Picasso *(p78)*. Housed in five graceful Gothic palaces on medieval Carrer de Montcada *(p83)*, the collection focuses mainly on the artist's early years. Afterwards, stop in at La Vinya del Senyor *(p83)* for a glass of wine; the best seats are on the terrace in front of Santa Maria del Mar *(p86)*, an exemplar of Catalan Gothic.

Evening For dinner, head to much-lauded Cal Pep *(p90)*. You could eat in the dinky dining area at the back, but the best seats are at the bar, where the congenial Pep keeps court. Fill up on *trifàsic* (a platter of fried calamari, whitebait and prawns) and *crema catalana*, a sort of crème brûlée. Follow up the feast with cocktails at Paradiso *(p83)*, a "secret" bar at the back of a pastrami bar. After such a glorious day, fall into bed at Banys Orientals *(p93)*.

Day 2

Morning Drift back in time wandering the enticing narrow streets of the medieval Barri Gòtic *(p98)*. Explore the ruins of old Bàrcino, the original Roman settlement, in the bowels of Museu d'Història de Barcelona *(p80)*; here remain streets rutted by Roman cartwheels and vats still stained with dye after two thousand years. Later, emerge, blinking into the light, and head down La Rambla, Barcelona's most famous promenade, to the glorious Boqueria market, properly known as Mercat de Sant Josep *(p72)*. The colourful stalls are a perfect opportunity to brighten any photo album – and there are inviting counter bars for a tasty lunch.

Afternoon After lunch head to Gaudí's awe-inspiring, albeit unfinished, Sagrada Família cathedral *(p106)* to marvel at the rainbow-tinted nave. Ascend the lift to the rooftop for spectacular views – and brace yourself for the vertiginous spiral staircase that will bring you back down. Seek refreshment on your return to ground level at Chill Bar *(p118)*, a friendly, arty little spot with a well-chosen wine list.

Evening Dine at Botafumeiro *(p159)*, one of Barcelona's best seafood restaurants, where long-aproned waiters bear platters of just-caught shellfish. After a postprandial stroll through Gràcia, catch a live gig at Heliogàbasl *(www.heliogabal.com)*, one of the city's smallest and most atmospheric music venues.

←

1 Clear skies above the curving spit of Garraf marina.

2 Glinting light over Tortosa's historical centre.

3 Exploring Tarragona's Roman history.

4 A table laden with freshly made *suquet de peix*.

3 DAYS

in southern Catalonia

Day 1

Morning Start things off with a leisurely walk around the old fishing village of Garraf, before heading into the wild with a hike through the *matollar (p188)* at nearby Parc Natural del Garraf. When you emerge from the wilderness, make a beeline for La Cúpula (*www.lacupulagarraf.com*) near the beach and experience what these coastal towns do best – seafood. Keep it Catalan with a *suquet de peix* (fish stew).

Afternoon The warm sea is perfect for a quick dip before the ten-minute train ride to lively Sitges *(p197)*. Wander through its charming narrow streets down to the seemingly endless Passeig Marítim promenade. Tear yourself away from the epic sea views to snap a picture of the impressive Sant Bartomeu i Santa Tecla.

Evening Indulge in tasty tapas plates at Komokieras *(p199)* in the Old Town, then return to the seafront for some beachside cocktails at Pub Voramar *(p197)*. As the night wears on, move the party to El Piano *(p197)* to round things off with live music and an unbeatable friendly atmosphere.

Day 2

Morning Breakfast in Sitges before catching a train to Tarragona to immerse yourself in the town's Roman ruins *(p174)*, a World Heritage Site. A walk past the Balcó del Mediterrani viewing point, where the vast ocean stretches away, takes you to the amphitheatre ruins, the epicentre of Roman Tarraco. Find a neighbourhood café for a leisurely *l'hora del vermut* (vermouth hour),

sipping the local drink and nibbling *seitons* (pickled sardines), a Catalan delicacy.

Afternoon Grab some *clotxa* (bread stuffed with herring, onions, tomatoes and garlic) from a stall along the Rambla Nova then dive into the winding streets of the Old Town for an on-the-spot tour of the fascinating Roman sights all around.

Evening Bring yourself back to the present day at laid-back A3Mans *(p175)*, where Catalan classics are given a contemporary twist. A restful night awaits at the Hotel Astari (*www.hotelastari.com*).

Day 3

Morning A classic tapas-style *esmorzar de forquilla* breakfast at Bar Cortijo (977 22 48 67) is perfect fuel for a jaunt to the Delta de l'Ebre *(p198)*, a paradise for nature lovers. Have your binoculars at the ready: birds flock here in their thousands. When hunger strikes, Lo Pati D'Agustí in tiny El Poblenou del Delta has delicious *rossejat*, a local speciality made with seafood and rice.

Afternoon Leave the park behind for historical Tortosa *(p198)*, a microcosm of Catalonian history. Explore the town's labyrinthine streets on foot, stopping first at the impressive cathedral where a Roman temple, a Moorish mosque and an earlier 12th-century cathedral have all stood.

Evening Before sunset make your way to the Castell de la Suda, the remnants of a Moorish fort. High above the town, it's a superb spot to watch dusk settle over the Río Ebre with a glass of wine in the parador that now occupies the ancient castle.

5 DAYS
in Barcelona and Catalonia

Day 1

Morning Set out on foot to get your bearings in Barcelona's medieval heart. The narrow streets of ancient El Born (p100) are awash with enticing boutiques and cafés. Stop at Satan's Coffee Corner (www. satanscoffee.com) for hellishly good coffee before turning down Carrer de Montcada (p83) to marvel at medieval mansions.

Afternoon Lunch on *pulpo al hierro* (grilled octopus) in the retro-chic Elsa y Fred (p90), then swing by the Palau de la Música Catalana (p76), a Modernista concert hall, to pick up tickets for later. Spend the afternoon at the arty MACBA (p83).

Evening After a music-filled evening, head down to the Eixample neighbourhood for reinterpreted Catalan cuisine at Casa Calvet (p117) – the dining rooms are designed by Gaudí. Finally, a sumptuous bed awaits at the Serras Hotel (p93).

Day 2

Morning Begin the day with a plunge in the hotel's rooftop pool, then stroll down the city's most famous road, La Rambla (p72), to Gaudí-designed Palau Güell (p74). Don't miss the rooftop, a forest of colourfully tiled chimneys – the photo opportunities are as epic as the views.

Afternoon Enjoy a traditional lunch at a counter bar in the Boqueria market (p72), then carry on up the Passeig de Gràcia to another Gaudí masterpiece, the fairy-tale Casa Batlló (p112), dubbed "the House of Bones" for its curiously shaped windows. Gaudí's rooftop was apparently inspired by the scaly back of the dragon killed by Sant Jordi, Catalonia's patron saint.

Evening Wander into the shadowy Montjuïc to rub shoulders with a loyal following of locals as you sample the menu of *montaditos* (tapas on bread) at Quimet i Quimet (p133); its 500-strong wine list means you'll always find a perfect pairing.

Day 3

Morning Leave the city behind for pretty, hilly Sant Pol de Mar (p192), a whitewashed maze behind a string of sandy beaches. Dip your toes in the sea, then window shop through chic boutiques and art galleries.

Afternoon For lunch tuck into rice dishes at seafront Banys Lluís *(www.banyslluis.cat)*. Then, follow the coast to clifftop Tossa de Mar *(p190)*, a well-preserved warren of whitewashed 13th-century lanes.

Evening Climb the narrow streets behind the marina to tiny La Lluna *(972 34 25 23)*, to feast on *sipia a la planxa* (pan-fried cuttlefish) and *rossejat negro* (squid-ink pasta with allioli), a Catalan speciality.

Day 4

Morning Follow the winding coastal road along the Costa Brava *(p191)*, past gorgeous turquoise coves, pausing in summer months for a dip in the sea.

Afternoon Arrive in Girona *(p172)* in time for a plate of *vegetals fideuà*, a vegetarian take on the Catalan paella with pasta at Amaranta *(www.amarantavegetal.cat)*. The old city's enticingly tangled streets, recognizable to *Game of Thrones* fans, are an easy place to get lost and found again.

Evening Splash out this evening at El Celler de Can Roca *(p173)* and follow the Roca brothers on a culinary adventure.

Tastebuds tingling, head back to a night at Hotel Històric *(www.hotelhistoric.com)*, in the heart of the Old Town.

Day 5

Morning Kick-start the day at Espresso Mafia *(www.espressomafiagirona.com)*; the expertly made coffee will power you to Figueres *(p187)*, 35 minutes north by train. Take a surreal turn at Salvador Dalí's eye-popping "theatre-museum", packed with his extraordinary artworks.

Afternoon Continue to picture-perfect Cadaqués *(p186)* and grab some *pa amb tomàquet* (garlicky, tomato-rubbed grilled bread) to take to the beach that dusts the tip of this wild and beautiful Cap de Creus headland. Dalí's former home in tiny Port Lligat offers a fascinating guided tour.

Evening As dusk settles make your way to harbour-front Casa Nun *(675 46 88 84)*. Ask for the romantic table on the tiny upstairs balcony and watch the boats bob in the harbour as you enjoy fresher-than-fresh seafood accompanied by sparkling cava and memories of the last five days.

On the Trail of Great Artists

The homes and haunts of some of Spain's most revered artists, including Pablo Picasso and Salvador Dalí, have been converted into museums where artworks are complemented by a fascinating glimpse into the artist's process. In Barcelona, check out the Els 4 Gats tavern *(www.4gats.com)* where Picasso held his first exhibition, then wander around its superb collection of the artist's early output. Across the city, marvel at Miró's colourful and unique style at the light-filled Fundació Joan Miró *(p128)*, which he designed with architect Josep Lluís Sert. Up the coast, get lost in the "Dalí Triangle" – comprising the Teatre-Museu in Figueres *(p187)*, his enchanting former home in Port Lligat and his wife Gala's medieval castle in Púbol – where Surrealist daydreams come to life.

$\rightarrow$

Admiring the vibrant tapestries at the Fundació Joan Miró

BARCELONA AND CATALONIA FOR
ART LOVERS

A dynamic hotbed of creativity for centuries, Catalonia is brimming with groundbreaking art. From remarkable Romanesque wall paintings in remote Pyrenean churches and Gothic masterpieces in world-class museums, to Barcelona's Modernisme marvels and the wild public art of Gaudí and Tàpies, discover the trove of Catalan art.

Take to the Streets

From murals to stunning statues, graffiti to light installations, Catalonia's public art is a great way to indulge in some culture on the cheap. Stroll Port Olímpic *(p91)* to see Roy Lichtenstein's colourful *Barcelona Head,* then head to the beach to take in Rebecca Horn's charming sculpture, *The Wounded Star.* In El Raval *(p82)* snap Fernando Botero's much-loved *Cat,* and in the Parc de Joan Miró *(p151)* take a selfie with the artist's curvaceous sculpture, *Woman and Bird.* These artworks are complemented by a vibrant street art scene: Bombcelona *(www.bombcelona.es)* highlights some of the city's best graffiti art.

$\leftarrow$

Roy Lichtenstein's pop art *Barcelona Head* sculpture in Port Olímpic

TOP 5 GALLERIES IN BARCELONA

CaixaForum
This converted factory hosts superb temporary exhibitions *(p132)*.

Fundació Joan Miró
The world's largest Miró collection in a stunning building *(p128)*.

Museu Can Framis
Contemporary Catalan art at a remodelled factory complex *(p157)*.

Foto Colectania
Photography exhibitions in a small gallery *(www.fotocolectania.org)*.

Projecte SD
Uptown gallery with a focus on artists' books *(www.projectesd.com)*.

← Honing skills with Life Drawing Barcelona

Creating Art

Each September, the Museu Picasso *(p78)* organizes the Big Draw, with drawing workshops hosted at venues across the city. During the rest of the year, try your hand at drawing with Life Drawing Barcelona *(www.lifedrawingbarcelona.com)*. Alternatively, capture the city on intensive weekend courses for beginners with Barcelona Photographer *(www.barcelonaphotographer.com)*.

World-Class Museums

Dip into Barcelona's glorious MNAC *(p130)* to admire Romanesque murals gathered here from remote Pyrenean churches and a millennium of Catalan art. The dazzling MACBA *(p83)* hosts world-class modern and contemporary art, including pieces by Antoni Tàpies. Further afield, the Thyssen-Bornemisza museum *(www.museothyssen.org)* in Sant Feliu de Guíxols has a fine collection of 19th- and 20th-century Catalan art.

←

The striking modern architecture of Barcelona's MACBA museum

On Fizz and Terroir

From earthy reds to fizzy cava, the wines of Catalonia make the taste buds sing. Tour the vineyards of Clos Figueras *(www.closfigueras.info)*, in the Tarragona province, then quaff a glass of red made from local Cariñena and Garnacha grapes. For something more bubbly, head to Penedès to tour some revered cava cellars, including Codorníu *(www.visitascodorniu.com)* with its charming Modernista cellar.

←

Wine tasting at the small Castell Roig winery in the Penedès region

BARCELONA AND CATALONIA FOR
FOODIES

Whether you're sampling avant-garde gastronomy, tucking into tasty home-cooking at a family-run country inn or just enjoying some mouthwatering sardines fresh from the grill by the beach, the culinary delights of Catalonia are a feast for both the belly and the soul.

TOP 5 CATALAN DISHES

Pa amb tomàquet
Bread rubbed with garlicky tomatoes and seasoned with olive oil.

Escudella i carn d'olla
A meat and vegetable stew with pasta or rice.

Esqueixada
A fresh salad with tomatoes and salted cod.

Coca Catalana
Flatbread served with any number of toppings.

Crema Catalana
Similar to crème brûlée, but with cinnamon and lemon zest.

Super Street Food

Street food fanatics head to Eat Street *(www.eatstreet.barcelona)*, hosted in a reused factory in Poble Sec, to sample tacos or ceviche sold from trucks. Across town, check out the trendy Palo Market Fest *(www.palomarketfest.com)*, or visit the Mercantic vintage market *(www.mercantic.com)* in Sant Cugat for Catalan classics.

→

Busy food stalls at Barcelona's monthly Palo Market Fest

Third-Wave Coffee Bars

Coffee culture has hit Catalonia in a big way, with Scandi style and the aroma of fresh-roasted beans wafting through hip coffee joints on every urban corner. Looking for Barcelona's best java, carefully roasted and brewed by meticulous baristas? Get your caffeine fix at Nømad *(www.nomadcoffee.es)* in El Born or Satan's Coffee Corner *(satanscoffee.com),* which has two outposts (one in the Gothic Quarter and one on the Eixample). In Girona, check out La Fábrica *(www. lafabricagirona.com)* on the edge of the Jewish Quarter.

↑ Enjoying a coffee break in a colourful Barcelona café

Nueva Cocina

Catalonia's "new cuisine" is the brainchild of chef Ferran Adrià, whose famed restaurant El Bulli *(www.elbullifoundation.com)* returns in 2019 as a "museum to culinary innovation". Peruse the on-site laboratory, then feast on the fare from kitchens run by Adrià's prodigies.

←

A creative dessert of chocolate bonbons and blackcurrant sorbet

Traditional Catalan Cuisine

Pa amb tomàquet (toasted bread rubbed with fresh tomato and drizzled with olive oil) is found every-where, from food stalls to gourmet restaurants. In Vic *(p193),* sample a platter of *embutits* (charcuterie) and tasty *escalivada* (garlicky roast aubergine and peppers). On the coast, try the local version of "surf 'n' turf", *sípia amb mandonguilles* (squid with meatballs).

→

Fried white beans and sausage, a typical Catalan dish

Awesome Entertainment

Take the kids up to Tibidabo *(p154)*, on the outskirts of Barcelona, for thrills and spills at one of Spain's oldest and prettiest funfairs while you soak up the views over Barcelona. Come evening, wow the kids with Montjuïc's Font Màgica *(p134)*, where dancing fountains are lit up with a colourful sound and light show – always a hit.

←

Young and old enjoying the spectacle at Montjuïc's Font Màgica

BARCELONA AND CATALONIA FOR
FAMILIES

In a country that welcomes children with open arms, Catalonia is a perfect family destination. An abundance of theme parks, castles and museums, waterfalls and nature reserves means there's something for everyone. The fun-packed Barcelona has it all, including almost 5 kilometres of city beaches.

TRAVELLING WITH YOUNG CHILDREN

Expect to see kids out and about until late, particularly during the summer. Barcelona's metro and bus network are almost completely pushchair-friendly, but you may struggle with the Old Town's cobbled streets. Bring a booster seat, as taxis rarely have them and they can double as highchairs. Getting around Barcelona can be fun: take a cable car to Montjuïc or a vintage tram up to Tibidabo.

Little Artists

The city that inspired Gaudí, Picasso and Miró has plenty to keep budding young artists happy. Enchanting Barcelona *(www.enchantingbarcelonatours.com)* run a family-friendly tour including a visit to the Museu Picasso and a painting workshop, where kids can create their own masterpieces.

→

Kids taking part in the Big Draw at the Museu Picasso

↑ Snapping photos for the family album at Park Güell in Barcelona

Open-Air Fun

Barcelona has play areas on virtually every block to help energetic kids burn off steam. Looking for more space to run wild? Head to Parc de la Ciutadella (p88), the city's largest green space, where you can also take a rowboat out on the lake. Park Güell is another great bet, combining a little culture with the great outdoors. Alternatively, venture into Val d'Aran (p179), in the Spanish Pyrenees, to play hide-and-seek in shady forested groves.

INSIDER TIP
Time for Dinner

Many restaurants don't open until 8:30 or 9pm, but there are tapas bars – with child-sized portions – to fill the gap. The city centre has restaurants that are open all day: look for signs saying *cocina interrumpida*.

Wet and Wild

When the summer months heat up, you can cool off at one of Catalonia's epic water parks. Slip down twisting water slides and splash in the wave pool at Illa Fantasia (www.illafantasia.com), the closest to Barcelona. Picnic areas and a free shuttle bus service from the city are handy perks. Further down the coast, make a splash at the Caribe Aquatic Park, part of Port Aventura (www.portaventura worldcom) theme park.

A thrilling ride at ↑ Port Aventura theme park

Great Bookshops

The main hub of the Spanish publishing industry, Catalonia has a fantastic array of enticing bookshops. In Barcelona, browse shelves of rare tomes at the Librería Anticuaria Farré; then cross the city to Altaïr *(p156)*, a charming bookshop-cum-café with a fantastic travel literature section.

$\longrightarrow$

Perusing the shelves in one of Catalonia's delightful bookshops

BARCELONA AND CATALONIA FOR
BOOKWORMS

Delve into Catalonia's rich literary history, which ranges from the chivalric madness of *Don Quixote* to the critically acclaimed exposé of the Spanish Civil War in *Homage to Catalonia*. Join Catalan bibliophiles at independent festivals, in quirky bookshops and on the hunt for literary locales.

Fiesta Time!

Book-loving Catalonia is a treat for bookworms, hosting scores of fabulous literary festivals throughout the year. One of the best is Kosmopolis *(www. kosmopolis.cccb.org)*, Barcelona's biennial festival hosted by the Centre de Cultura Contemporània de Barcelona; meet top writers from around the world, attend author panels and discover what's hot on the literary stage. On La Diada de Sant Jordi (23 April), which is Catalonia's literary answer to Valentine's Day, exchange books with the one you love.

$\longleftarrow$

Street atmosphere during Barcelona's biennial Kosmopolis festival

Homage to Barcelona

Few cities have captured the imagination quite like the Catalan capital. Let Colm Toibin's *Homage to Barcelona* lead you through the best of its art and architecture. Dive down a different alley with Manuel Vázquez Montalbán's series, featuring the gourmet detective Pepe Carvalho. Use the story as inspiration for a Catalan feast across the city.

→

Barcelona-born writer and journalist Manuel Vázquez Montalbán

The Shadow of the Wind (Carlos Ruiz Zafón)

This tour-de-force describes a young boy's discovery of a unique book in the Cemetery of Lost Books.

Homage to Catalonia (George Orwell)

A riveting and widely read account of Orwell's experiences fighting for the Republicans during the bloody Spanish Civil War.

Cathedral of the Sea (Ildefonso Falcones)

This dreamy novel recounts the long construction of the beautiful church of Santa Maria del Mar.

Plaça de Catalunya, one of Barcelona's literary locales ↓

Literary Tours

Books come to life in the streets of Barcelona through the fantastic self-guided literary tours created by Barcelona's tourist office *(www.barcelonaturisme.com)*. Our favourite takes in all the locations featured in George Orwell's *Homage to Catalonia*. Led by literary historians, conèixerBcn *(www.coneixerbcn.com)* also runs excellent guided literary tours focusing on Catalan classics, such as *The Shadow of the Wind* by Carlos Ruiz Zafón.

Driving the Cadafalch

With neo-Gothic spikes and sculptures, Josep Puig i Cadafalch's architecture recalls Catalonia's glory years in the Middle Ages, when it ruled a vast Mediterranean empire. Check out the imposing façade of Casa Terrades, which has needle-thin turrets *(119).* Cadafalch designed Casa Amatller, the home of wealthy chocolatier Antoni Amatller i Costa, to resemble a Gothic palace but, covered in sculptures of animals making and eating chocolate, this building differs from his other designs. Take a tour of the residence, climbing the grand staircase to the family's private apartments, before dipping a biscotti into a steaming cup of hot chocolate.

→

The fortress-like exterior of Cadalfalch's Casa Terrades, with its soaring spires

BARCELONA AND CATALONIA FOR
MODERNISTA MARVELS

Modernisme – sometimes called Catalan Art Nouveau – transformed Barcelona's skyline between the late 19th and early 20th centuries. Although Gaudí is the best-known proponent of the style, Lluís Domènech i Montaner and Josep Puig i Cadafalch also left their marks on the city.

Oh My Gaudí!

From the vast, as yet unfinished, spires of the Sagrada Família *(p106)* to the luxuriant gardens of the Park Güell *(p144),* guarded by a pair of fairy-tale pavilions, Gaudí is every-where you look in Barcelona. As well as these large-scale public works, he designed scores of imaginative private homes for wealthy patrons and there are equally inventive ways to visit each of them. Sip a glass of cava to the sound of a string quartet on the otherworldly roof of Palau Güell *(p74),* take an augmented reality tour of Casa Batlló *(p112)* or join Gaudí himself – or Mrs Ramoneta, the family's maid – on a kids' tour of La Pedrera, with an actor *(p114).*

→

Overlooking the city from Gaudí's psychedelically tiled bench, Park Güell

Climbing the Montaner

Lluís Domènech i Montaner is often described as the father of Modernisme. He designed two of Barcelona's most glorious buildings – the Palau de la Música Catalana *(p76)* and Hospital de la Santa Creu i de Sant Pau *(p118)*. Guided tours are available for both of these buildings, but catching a concert under the stained glass in the Palau de la Música Catalana or in the grand gardens of what is now the Sant Pau Recinte Modernista is an absolutely unforgettable experience.

←

Statues of muses on a mosaicked wall in the Palau de la Música Catalana

DRINK

Els 4 Gats

Picasso's favourite watering hole has grand Modernista proportions.

⌂ Carrer de Montsió
W 4gats.com

London Bar

Enjoy a tipple under this tiny bar's sweeping signage. Delectable tapas accompanies glistening glasses here.

⌂ Carrer Nou de la Rambla 34 W london
bar-bar.negocio.site

Café de l'Òpera

Once La Mallorquina chocolate shop, this café has mirrors decorated with characters from different operas.

⌂ La Rambla 74
W cafeoperabcn.com

↑ The blue-tiled light well in Gaudí's Casa Batlló

Ruta del Modernisme

As well as covering the big-name sights – and entitling you to discounts – this self-guided walking tour will lead you to the city's hidden Modernista gems *(www.rutadelmodernisme.com)*. Pick up a guide from any of Barcelona's tourist offices and follow the red plaques to some of the 120 buildings. Browse the wooden shelves of the charming Farmàcia Bolós *(Rambla de Catalunya 77)*, after snapping a picture of its stained-glass doorway, or admire the cathedral-like Casa Martí before enjoying a tipple in the tiled Els 4 Gats on the ground floor.

Kilometre Zero

The "kilometre zero" concept grew out of the slow food movement: the premise is to produce, sell and eat locally grown and sourced food. You'll see signs in shops and restaurants where Kilometre Zero (often shortened to "KM0") food is available. Good bets for finding KM0 food in Barcelona include the small Flax & Kale restaurant group and Gat Blau in the Sant Antoni neighbourhood.

←

Fine dining in Barcelona's restaurants linked to the slow food movement

BARCELONA AND CATALONIA
THINK GREEN

The Catalan capital has proved its commitment to sustainability, from promoting public transport and cycling to establishing a sustainability education centre. Elsewhere in Catalonia, there are organic and biodynamic farms, wineries and olive-oil producers, and farmer's markets in many towns.

EAT

Rasoterra
Tuck into innovative veggie and vegan dishes at this slow-food favourite.

🏠 Carrer Palau 5
🌐 rasoterra.cat

€€€

Flax & Kale Passage
Delicious and nutritious veggie and vegan food served in a chic setting.

🏠 Carrer de Sant Pere Més Alt 31–33
🌐 teresacarles.com/fk

€€€

Two Wheels
Barcelona has about 300 km (186 miles) of bike paths stretching across the city, part of a broad initiative backed by the city to make it greener, less polluted and quieter. Among the scores of places that rent bikes is Un Cotxe Menys *(biketoursbarce lona.com)*, which means "one less car". Bikes are allowed on regional trains so you can also travel easily around Catalonia.

→

Cycling along the broad Passeig Marítim de la Barceloneta

Biodynamic Wineries

Catalan wines have enjoyed a renaissance over the last few decades, and the most recent shift has been towards more organic and biodynamic wines, often produced by small, boutique wineries. Biodynamic farming is a holistic way of production that goes beyond organic farming and aims to improve the land. Many producers are happy to invite visitors for tastings. You can also take a tour, such as the ones offered by Feel By Doing *(feelby doing.com)* including grape harvesting, vineyard picnics plus artisan cheeses and organic wine tasting.

↑ Authentic Catalan winery experiences on a tour with Feel By Doing

Plastic-Free Shopping

Across Barcelona you'll find several waste-free shops where you can bring your own containers to fill with goodies. Among them are the Yes Future Positive Supermarket *(www.yesfuture.store)* in Sant Antoni and Gra de Gràcia's three stores in Gràcia.

←

Bring-your-own-container shopping at Yes Future Positive Supermarket

Eco-Tours

These days tour companies are offering trips around Barcelona and Catalonia that focus on sustainability. Among them is El Brogit *(www. elbrogit.com)*, which runs a wide range of guided and self-guided tours including hiking, biking, star-gazing, photography, and visits to organic and biodynamic wine and olive oil producers.

→

Visiting local producers on an eco-tour with El Brogit

Spectacular Panoramas

After a day of sightseeing, get above the crowds at Bunkers del Carmel, a Civil War-era anti-aircraft battery. Tucked away in a quiet suburb, it's the perfect spot to relax over a glass of fizzing cava and views of the city lights as the sun sets.

There are more gorgeous, Barcelona-wide views to be had from the Torre Bellesguard (p155), the less famous sibling to Gaudí's La Pedrera.

People taking in the impressive city views at Bunkers del Carmel ↑

BARCELONA AND CATALONIA
OFF THE BEATEN TRACK

Barcelona's extraordinary history and idiosyncratic style can overshadow the wealth of unexpected gems waiting to be found across Catalonia. Whether you're after a tour with a twist or an escape into solitude, here we uncover the best of Catalonia's hidden treasures.

TOP 3 PARKS AND NATURE RESERVES

Serra de Collserola
Delicious, shady wilderness in the hills behind Barcelona (www.parcnatural collserola.cat).

Parc Nacional d'Aigüestortes
The only national park (p180) in Catalonia, set high in the Pyrenees, with spectacular lakes and waterfalls.

Zona Volcànica de la Garrotxa
Hiking paths and green, long-extinct volcanoes set in forest (www. parcsnaturals.gencat. cat/ca/garrotxa).

Templar Treasures

In the Middle Ages, the Knights Templar owned vast swathes of territory in Catalonia. Take the ferry across the Ebro to marvel at their castle at Miravet - one of the largest and best preserved in Europe, attesting to their extraordinary power. The order was disbanded by the pope in 1312, but you can track down more Templar remains in Tortosa (p198), where the castle is now a parador, and Lleida (p196), where Castell Templer de Gardeny has a fascinating museum of the knights' history.

The Art of Death

More marvellous than macabre, two cemeteries in Barcelona stand out for their extraordinary funerary art. The Montjuïc cemetery is replete with lavish, Modernista tombs; pay your respects to Joan Miró and other luminaries. The Neo-Classical Poblenou cemetery has beautiful sculptures; look out for Jaume Barba's *Petó de la Mort* (*Kiss of Death,* 1930).

→

The *Kiss of Death* marble sculpture located at El Poblenou cemetery

Quirky Tours

Take to the skies in a hot-air balloon tour with Vol de Coloms (*www.voldecoloms.cat*) to see the extraordinary volcanic landscape of the Garrotxa from above. If a tour on water is more your thing, enjoy a cruise through pink clouds of flamingos in the Delta de l'Ebre (*www.creuersdeltaebre.com*).

←

Gorgeous flamingos in the Delta de l'Ebre nature reserve

↑ The Knights Templar castle at Miravet on the Ebro river

Eccentric Collectors

The sculptor Frederic Marès gathered an extraordinary collection of curios, now beautifully displayed in the Museu Frederic Marès (*p81*). In nearby Sitges, the hotchpotch of items in the Museu del Cau Ferrat (*p197*) was brought together by Modernista artist Santiago Rusiñol.

↑ Ancient sculptures in the Museu Frederic Marès

Ode to the Setting Sun

To memorialize the golden hour in Barcelona, you need to head to the hills. You'll get some of the best panoramic shots of the city from the ramparts of Castell de Montjuïc *(p138)*, in the west, where you can place other landmarks in the frame. For stunning rooftop views from the heart of the city, climb up to the walkways above the Catedral de Barcelona *(p70)* – the carved stone of the central spire radiates warmth in the glow of the setting sun, a fantastic juxtaposition to the metal girders of the walkway. Down the coast, in Tarragona, crouch in the shadow of the slopes to use the setting sun to silhouette the soaring arches of the iconic Les Ferreres Aqueduct.

The golden hour in the Catalan capital ↑

BARCELONA AND CATALONIA FOR
PHOTOGRAPHERS

Catalonia is a nirvana for shutterbugs, all dreamy landscapes and stunning architecture. Its photogenic streets and dramatic vistas are the perfect backdrop for its colourful culture. All you need is a camera.

Lights, Camera, Capture!

As dusk falls, Barcelona becomes a sea of twinkling lights, adding a dreamlike quality to any snap. Set your shutter speed for a long exposure to get fluid, draping shots of fountains like Font Màgica *(p134)* – lit with brilliant colour, it's majestic at night. Climb to the rooftop of Las Arenas, in Plaça d'Espanya *(p138)*, and use the same technique with a tripod, for a fleeting shot of the vehicles whizzing around the central roundabout below.

→

The Font Màgica in Montjuïc, impressively lit up at night

Pickup By:
1/29/2024

C
A
M
P

8407

*

A Slice of Life

Catalonia's streetscapes are made for photography. In Barcelona use the buildings around the cathedral as an intriguing frame; Carrer del Dr Joaquim Pou is the most picturesque. Then head to La Rambla *(p72)* and let the bustling scene unfold before you. In Calella de Palafrugell, you'll find dazzling white houses and rustic fishermen's cottages. Idle on Port Bo, at the curving beach, to snap the catch-of-the-day being hauled up onto shore.

↓ Fishing boats stranded on Barques beach in Calella de Palafrugell

Gaudí Inside and Out

Synonymous with Catalan Modernisme, Gaudí's buildings are achingly photogenic. The immense, far-from-complete Sagrada Família *(p106)* is emblematic of his signature style. Snap its exterior from Plaça de Gaudí across the road, where the cathedral is perfectly mirrored in a small lake. At Casa Batlló *(p112)* go inside, wide-angle lens at the ready, to capture its fantastic interiors.

←

Jesus on the cross above the altar of the majestic Sagrada Família cathedral

Enter the Heartland

Rural Catalonia offers shutterbugs spectacular scenery, from picturesque villages where time seems to stand still to stunning mountainscapes. Follow the trail cut into cliffs above the Congost de Mont-rebei to frame images of the gorge and the river below - for a dramatic sense of scale, try to catch someone walking along the path. Later, go south to Penedès for the perfect symmetry of hills corduroyed with vineyards, then pause for a while at El Pinell de Brai, one of the town's epic wine cathedrals *(p195)*.

→

Kayaking in the dramatic Congost de Mont-rebei

Wonderful Wetlands

Catalonia has two extensive marshlands that are home to an extraordinary array of bird life. Bring your binoculars to the Parc Natural dels Aiguamolls de l'Empordà *(www.parcsnaturals.gencat. cat/ca/aiguamolls-emporda)*, a mosaic of marshland, lagoons and dunes on the Costa Brava, to spot white storks and Cetti's warbler from bird hides and a viewing tower. The Delta de l'Ebre *(p198)* protects a landscape of endless beaches, rice fields and marshes. Cruise it with a shallow-bottomed punt from Lo Mas de la Cuixota *(www. lomasdelacuixota.com)* and see the mesmeric dance of resident flamingos up close.

↑ A beautiful flock of flamingos in the Delta de l'Ebre marshes

CATALONIA FOR
WILD SPACES

Catalonia is home to a vast array of landscapes, with plenty of opportunities to get into the wild. Hike or sail around wild headlands, watch myriad birds in beautiful wetlands, dive in pristine waters, star-gaze in remote canyons or try your hand at mushrooming (a Catalan passion). The choice is yours.

"Twisted Waters"

Catalonia's only national park, the Parc Nacional d'Aigüestortes *(p180)* encompasses gorgeous scenery. Set your sights on the hundreds of miles of "twisted waters" – the streams and waterfalls tumbling through its meadows and valleys. Glorious for a spot of wild swimming, these pristine waterways also offer prime wildlife watching opportunities, including the elusive brown bear. Less than 40 km (25 miles) southeast, Paddle in Spain *(www.paddlein spain.com)* runs kayaking trips for the whole family down the Río Noguera Pallaresa.

←

The emerald waters of Estany Tort de Peguera in Parc Nacional d'Aigüestortes

Sky High

Looming over the northern edge of Catalonia, the Pyrenees mountain range is criss-crossed with perfect ski slopes. Snow bunnies will have a fantastic time at Boí Taüll *(www.boitaullresort.com)*, the highest ski slopes in the Pyrenees at a soaring 2,751 m (9,025 ft), which transform into tranquil hiking and cycling trails come summer. In the Montsec mountain range, an hour outside Lleida on Catalonia's western border, you can hike across dramatic *congostos* (gorges) carved into the mountains. Arguably the most dramatic is the Congost de Mont-rebei, a dizzying trail etched into the cliffside. Since 2013 Montsec has been designated a Starlight Reserve area - one of only six in the world, it boasts exceptional conditions for enjoying the starlight. After enjoying a long day of hiking, galactic panoramas await during a guided nighttime visit to the Parc Astronòmic del Montsec *(www.parcastronomic.cat)*, thanks to the retractable cupola at the observatory.

← The multimedia planetarium at the Parc Astronòmic del Montsec

TOP 3 **HIKING TRAILS**

Sitges to Vilanova i la Geltrú
Enjoy a stroll along the clifftops between Sitges *(p197)* and Vilanova i la Geltrú, stopping off for a refreshing dip.

Trans-Pyrenean Hike (GR11)
A demanding and immensely rewarding hike, this spans the Pyrenees to the Basque Lands, beginning in Cadaqués *(p186)*.

Montserrat
Most famous for its basilica, Montserrat *(p168)* also offers panoramic hiking and climbing routes.

Into the Woods

Catalonia is swathed in ancient forests, protected by national parks. Hike in the undulating landscape formed by long-extinct volcanoes in the Zona Volcànica de la Garrotxa *(www.gencat.cat/parcs/garrotxa)*, covered in forests. Return in autumn with a camera to capture the Fageda d'en Jordà, a majestic beech forest growing on a plain formed by an ancient lava flow from the Croscat volcano.

← The lush, forested landscape of the Fageda d'en Jordà and La Garrotxa

Medieval Mercantile Empire

Barcelona was the centre of a vast empire built on maritime trade that stretched as far as Sicily and Greece during the Middle Ages. Huge galleys were built in the Drassanes (shipyards), now converted into the excellent Maritime Museum *(p96)*. The church of Santa Maria del Mar *(p86)* was built with donations by local merchants and shipbuilders.

$\rightarrow$

The striking façade of the Gothic Basílica de Santa Maria del Mar

BARCELONA AND CATALONIA FOR
HISTORY BUFFS

Phoenicians, Greeks, Romans and many other peoples have left their mark in Catalonia. From the ancient Greek settlement of Empúries to the splendid royal mausoleum at Poblet, the region is rich in historic treasures, while Barcelona's Gothic Quarter is one of the largest surviving medieval cities in Europe.

CATALONIA'S INDEPENDENCE MOVEMENT

In the early 18th century, the Catalans backed the losing side in the Spanish War of Succession, and Barcelona fell after a 14-month-long siege. The Bourbon victors abolished Catalan rights and institutions; a huge swathe of the El Born neighbourhood was demolished and a vast fortress built in its place. The ruins dating from this period have been preserved in the excellent Born Cultural and Memorial Centre, which is now ground zero for the Catalan independence movement.

Spanish Civil War

There are, thankfully, few vestiges of the devastating Spanish Civil War in Catalonia, but you can visit a bomb shelter in Poble Sec, while the anti-aircraft battery on the Turó de la Rovira is now a cultural centre. Nick Lloyd runs a superb Civil War tour *(info@spanishcivilwartours.com)* for history buffs.

$\rightarrow$

Enjoying Barcelona views from the Turó de la Rovira anti-aircraft battery

> **Did You Know?**
>
> An estimated 45,000 foreign nationals came to Catalonia to help in the fight against Franco.

The Olympic Effect

The 1992 Olympic Games, held in Barcelona, were responsible not just for putting the city firmly on the tourist map but for pulling Spain out of its Francoist isolationism. Barcelona was transformed: the rotting warehouses that used to line the seafront were replaced with a pleasure port (the Port Olímpic) and a new residential district (the Vila Olímpica) and many sporting facilities were built. Relive the 1992 Games at the enjoyable Olympic Museum *(p138)* on Montjuïc.

→

The bright lights of Port Olímpic's promenade at night

Extraordinary Cave Art

Discover a remarkable record of early humanity across Catalonia. In the Delta de l'Ebre *(p198)* you can see more than 400 dynamic sketches of hunting and battle; start at the interactive Abrics de l'Ermita visitors' centre at Ulldecona. In the Roca dels Moros *(p196),* near Lleida, male and female figures dance in vivid red and black, hair whipping with energy as animals look on.

←

Vivid prehistoric rock painting in the Roca dels Moros

Roman Barcino

The remains of the Roman settlement of Barcino can be seen beneath the MUHBA *(p80)* in the old town, the cart-rutted streets still redolent after two millennia. The columns of the once majestic Temple of Augustus still stand, engulfed in the medieval walls, as well as ancient Roman sarcophagi in the Plaça de la Vila de Madrid.

→

The ancient Roman columns of the Temple of Augustus

The Rhythm Takes Control

Beloved by Catalans, flamenco *tablaos* (literally "flamenco floorboard") attract aficionados across Barcelona and beyond. Head to the Tablao Flamenco Cordobés *(www.tablao cordobes.es)* and El Patio Andaluz *(www.show flamencobarcelona.com)* to see some of the best flamenco dancers in action.

An emotional live performance at the Tablao Flamenco Cordobés

BARCELONA AND CATALONIA
AFTER DARK

Vivacious by day, Barcelona really lights up after sunset. From underground clubs to cocktails with a view, the city's got you covered. Outside the capital, Girona has a vibrant party scene, Sitges is an LGBT+ hotspot and, in summer, the seaside resorts fill up as people flock to to the sands to dance till dawn.

TOP 3 NIGHTLIFE ON THE COSTA BRAVA

Lloret de Mar
Quiet by day, the beaches and bars of Lloret de Mar (one of the busiest resorts on the "wild coast") break loose as soon as the sun sets.

Begur
This sun-drenched coastal town shines after dark, especially at popular dusk-till-dawn spot La Lluna *(972 62 20 23)*.

Platja d'Aro
As the stars emerge, bars spill onto the beach and dance club Mala Vida *(651 84 04 98)* draws night owls like moths to a flame.

Full of Pride

Cornerstones of Catalonia's gay scene, Barcelona and Sitges are the destinations for LGBT+ nightlife. Pick from scores of fantastic gay-friendly bars and clubs in Barcelona's "Gaixample" *(p116)*. Sitges's Pride parade takes fun into the stratosphere; the sleepy town is chock-a-block with LGBT+ spots – the best are clustered around Carrer de Joan Tarrida.

Revellers fill the streets for Sitges's Pride parade

Music in the Air

In the summer months through to September, grab a glass of perfectly chilled cava and catch jazz concerts on the spectacular rooftop of La Pedrera *(p114)*, flanked by stunning citywide views. On ground level, take a picnic supper and a blanket to lay on the grass in municipal parks across the city. You can enjoy the strands of classical music (and occasionally jazz or blues) wafting on the evening breeze as part of the Música als Parcs programme held from June to August.

↑ The Sey Sisters performing during the Música als Parcs event

Jazz in the Night

Barcelona's jazz scene is legendary. Jazz lovers flock into town during the Barcelona Jazz Festival *(www.jazz.barcelona)* in October to see some of the world's greatest talent play across the city. Alternatively, catch fantastic live bands at iconic Harlem *(www.harlemjazzclub.es)*, or hop over to Girona's Sunset Jazz Club *(www.sunset jazz-club.com)* for some of the finest Catalan jazz.

← A jazz band on stage at Barcelona's Harlem club

Mixology Masters

Catalonia has long been home to potent liquors, from ratafia to vermouth. Learn how to shake, stir and whip these herb-infused brews into ever-creative concoctions at Collage Art & Cocktails Social Club *(www. collagecocktailbar.com)*, in a class taught by master mixologists, then sample the results. Outside Barcelona, let someone else do the work at gastro-cocktail chillout El Jardí de Can Marc *(www. canmarc.cat)* in Begur where divine drinks are served with stunning views.

→ A creative cocktail from Barcelona's Collage Art & Cocktails Social Club

Get Up to Speed

From motorbikes to rallycross, motorsport has left its mark in Catalonia. Join fans in April to cheer on rallycross competitors at the Circuit de Barcelona-Catalunya *(www.circuitcat.com)* in Montmeló. In May, embrace your inner speed demon at the Spanish Grand Prix. The F1 race used to wind through the roads of Montjuïc in Barcelona; the glory years are now evoked in the Espíritu de Montjuïc *(www.espiritu demontjuic.com)* in February.

→

Racing cars lining up for the Espíritu de Montjüic

BARCELONA AND CATALONIA FOR
SPORTS FANS

Sports-mad Catalans have more than just FC Barcelona to choose from. Locals are just as likely to cheer on their volleyball and basketball teams, embrace the need for speed at the Spanish Grand Prix, spend winter weekends zipping down Pyrenees slopes or dive into watersports all summer long.

Snow Party

When the mercury drops, Catalans flock to ski resorts dotted across the Catalan Pyrenees. Go full glam at Baqueira-Beret *(p178)*, where you might find yourself sharing the piste with Spanish royalty. Travelling with the kids? Get them out on the bunny slopes or making friends and snowmen at family-friendly Vall de Núria *(www. valldenuria.cat)*; the resort has a host of activities for all ages.

→

Heading for the slopes at the popular Baqueira-Beret resort

Wet, Wet, Wet

The stunning Mediterranean coastline offers a superb range of aquatic activities. Try your hand at paddle-boarding anywhere in the calm seas along the Costa Brava, then cross over to the marine nature reserve of the Illes Medes on the Costa Brava to dive beneath the waves with Aquàtica *(www.aquatica-sub.com)*. Alternatively, you can take a sailing lesson offered by Barcelona Sailing School *(www.barcelonasailingschool.com)*, which is based in the very marina built for the 1992 Olympics.

← Scuba diving off the Illes Medes on the Costa Brava

TOP 4 **TRAILS FOR RUNNING AND CYCLING**

Carretera de las Aigües
This track above Barcelona is the top spot for running and biking.

Banyoles
A lake ringed by a path perfect for gentle, family strolls or bike rides.

Montserrat
The "jagged mountain" has some challenging mountain biking routes.

Montseny
A leafy nature reserve with wonderful biking and running routes.

GREAT VIEW
See the City From a Pool

The Piscina Municipal de Montjuïc is an outdoor pool with staggering city-wide views. It is one of the sporting venues built for the 1992 Olympic Games, when it hosted the diving events.

Beautiful Games

Catalonia is football mad. While there are local teams and leagues across the province, Barça, as FC Barcelona *(www.fcbarcelona.com)* is commonly known, is the stuff of footballing legend. Grab tickets for a home game at Camp Nou *(p146)*, Europe's biggest stadium, then visit the on-site museum and admire the glittering trophies.

→ Passionate FC Barcelona fans at Camp Nou

Sand in the City

Bang in the heart of Barcelona, the Barceloneta is the perfect city break beach. Dotted with *xiringuitos* (beach bars), it has sun loungers for rent and scores of bars and restaurants within easy reach. South of the capital, L'Arrabassada has Blue Flag seas, golden sands and a promenade with little pop-ups perfect for picking up a refreshing *granizado de limon* (a lemon slushy).

←

The famous golden sands of the Platja de l'Arrabassada on the Costa Daurada

BARCELONA AND CATALONIA FOR
BEACHES

Catalonia's 800 kilometres of coastline are dotted with breathtaking beaches, from endless sweeps of golden sand to magical turquoise coves. Beaches for chilling, beaches for partying, beaches for families, and beaches for water-sports – you'll find them all along this gorgeous stretch of the Mediterranean.

Escape the Crowds

Escape to scores of tiny untouched coves tucked into the ochre cliffs of Catalonia's rugged coast. Find a quiet spot in the camping grounds outside Tossa de Mar, then hike the coastal path to Cala Llevadó, a sandy haven wedged between sea and pine woodland. Alternatively, you can walk the Camí de Ronda from Tamariu to reach the perfectly pebbly shores of secluded Cala Marquesa.

→

A motorboat lolling in the turquoise sea cove of Cala Marquesa

LGBT+ Beaches

All the beaches in Barcelona are gay-friendly, but Mar Bella is the best. Its stylish *xiringuitos* (bars) have live DJs and a party atmosphere all summer. In Sitges, our pick is Bassa Rodona, the main gay beach. The cliff walk south of the city has a couple of fab beach bars, perfect for cocktails and sea views.

INSIDER TIP
Camins de Ronda

Walking the scenic paths known as *camins de Ronda* is a great way to explore the stunning Catalan coastline, whether you opt for a leisurely hour's stroll or a week-long hike.

↑ The buzzing Bassa Rodona beach in Sitges

Fun for the Family

The pretty little beach of Garraf is a great option for kids, with pedaloes and rock pools; it's easily reached by train from Barcelona. On the Costa Brava, head to Tamariu's shallow beach flanked by pine-shaded cliffs or the endless, sugary sands of Platja Canadell in Calella de Palafrugell.

←

Calella de Palafrugel's large Platja del Canadell, popular with families

Beach Activities

Many of Barcelona's beaches offer watersports facilities; the Nova Icària beach, next to the Port Olímpic, has beach volleyball pitches and a city-run sailing school (www.vela barcelona.com). On the Costa Brava, pick up the paddles with Kayaking Costa Brava (www.kayakingcostabrava. com) to reach hidden coves.

→

Kayaking adventures along the Costa Brava

Of Giants and Fatheads

Catalan *gegants* (giants) and their sidekicks, the *capgrosses* (fatheads) have formed part of local festivities since the Middle Ages. Made of wood and papier-mâché, the *gegants* usually depict historical figures and dance in festival parades. The *capgrosses*, often caricatures of contemporary figures, create havoc for laughs. Get up close to these uncanny creations at La Casa dels Gegants in Lleida, then see them in action at Festa Major in May.

→

Traditional Catalan *gegants* parade through Barcelona

BARCELONA AND CATALONIA FOR
TRADITIONS

From fire-running to fatheads, human castles to the "dance of death", Catalan traditions are testament to the region's authentic culture. Experience it all across the region in fun-filled festas and unexpected rituals that date back hundreds of years.

TÍO DE NADAL

Every December, the kids in Catalonia bring out Tío de Nadal – a log painted with a smiling face that is usually wearing a jaunty *barretina* (the red Catalan beret) – and they fatten it up by "feeding" it vegetables. On Christmas Eve, a blanket is thrown over Tío de Nadal and the children beat the log with a stick while singing a traditional song that urges it to "poo" out sweets. The blanket is whipped away to reveal small gifts and *turrones* (traditional Catalan nougat, which is served at Christmas).

Firestarters

Easily the most spectacular event at any local festival, *correfoc* (fire-running) has its roots in pagan rituals. Join the crowd-packed streets as fire-spitting dragons lumber along, surrounded by leaping packs of *demonis* (demons) holding sparklers and Catherine wheels that whizz out fiery little sparks. Be sure to dress in old clothing and don't forget to cover any exposed skin.

→

Fun times during a Catalan fire-running performance

The Band Plays On

Catalonia's national dance emerged in earnest during the Renaixença. Look for it at any *festa*, as *sardanistas* (dancers) link hands with raised arms, forming circles that grow bigger and bigger as more people join in. When the circle gets too big, the dancers form more circles. Circles usually break off for novices, so you can join in as the cobla band plays on. Too shy to give it a go? Head to Montjuïc *(p124),* where you can practise your moves with the marvellous Monument a La Sardana, a ring of stone dancers commemorating solidarity.

←

Catalans performing the *sardana*

TOP 3 **TRADITIONAL FESTIVALS**

Patum de Berga (end of June)
Drums beat and townspeople dressed as mythical beasts dance through Berga in this ancient festival.

Dansa de la Mort (Easter week)
The Dance of Death in Verges is part of the town's Easter celebrations.

Corpus Christi (June)
The feast of Corpus Christi is beautifully celebrated with elaborately designed "carpets" of flowers in Sitges.

Race to the Top

Nothing encapsulates the egalitarian spirit of the Catalans like the *castellers,* teams of townspeople who stand on each other's shoulders in an effort to build the highest *castell* (human tower). Cheer them all the way to the top in Vilafranca del Penedès at the town festival in August or during Barcelona's La Mercè festival in September.

↑ Human towers built by teams of locals during Barcelona's city holiday, La Mercè

A YEAR IN
BARCELONA AND CATALONIA

JANUARY

△ **Els Tres Tombs** (*17 Jan*). Pets are blessed in honour of St Anthony, patron saint of animals.

Gran Festa de la Calçotada (*end Jan*). The air fills with the scent of grilling *calçots* (spring onions); eat them off a clay roof tile with Romanesco sauce.

FEBRUARY

Santa Eulàlia (*mid-Feb*). A light show, dancing and *gegant* (giant) parades honour the patron saint of Barcelona in the Old Town.

△ **Carnestoltes** (*late Feb*). All of Catalonia erupts in a confetti of sequins, feathers and fun to celebrate *dijous gras* (Mardi Gras).

MAY

△ **Fira de Sant Ponç** (*11 May*). Stock up on aromatic and medicinal herbs and honey at this ancient tradition on Barcelona's Carrer de l'Hospital.

Nit dels Museus (*18 May*). Nights at the museum are possible across Barcelona, in celebration of International Museums Day.

JUNE

Corpus Christi (*May/Jun*). Lay flowers and dance with *la patum* (dragon) in Berga to honour the Eucharist.

Primavera Sound (*late May–early Jun*). World-famous music acts up the tempo across the city.

△ **Sónar** (*Jun/Jul*) Let the DJ save your life (and then dance till dawn) at Barcelona's biggest electronic music festival, with bumper cars and more.

SEPTEMBER

Mostra del vi de l'Empordà (*1st weekend*). Raise a glass to Figueres's exquisite wine heritage, with workshops, vineyard tours and tastings.

△ **La Diada** (*11 Sep*). Catalonia's national day mourns its lost autonomy and celebrates Catalan identity.

La Mercè (*24 Sep*). Barcelona's annual festival honours *Nostra Senyora de la Mercè* (Our Lady of Mercy) in a week of concerts, masses and dances.

OCTOBER

△ **Concurs de Castells** (*early Oct*). Cheer on as *castellers* (human towers) triumph in Tarragona.

Sitges Film Festival (*early Oct*). Actors and directors flock to celebrate the fantasy genre.

Cavatast (*1st weekend*). Corks are popped across Catalonia in this effervescent festival.

El Festival Internacional de Jazz de Barcelona (*late Oct*). Join the hottest ticket in international jazz.

MARCH

De Cajón! Flamenco Festival *(Feb–Mar)*. *Bailaors* and *bailaoras* (flamenco dancers) stamp-tap through concerts and classes held in venues across Barcelona.

Festa de Sant Medir *(3 Mar)*. The sweetest festival of the year, with epic parades in Barcelona's Gràcia district that pepper the crowds with free sweets.

△ **Jazz Terrassa** *(two weeks mid-Mar)*. Music lovers get into the groove at this internationally renowned festival, with jazz concerts in venues around the village of Terrassa.

APRIL

Setmana Santa *(Mar–Apr)*. All across Catalonia, villages and towns erupt in Holy Week events in the seven days leading up to Easter.

△ **La Diada de Sant Jordi** *(23 Apr)*. Roses and books are exchanged during the Feast of St George, patron saint of Catalonia, known locally as *el dia del llibre* (book day).

Feria de Abril *(end Apr)*. Barcelona's Parc del Fòrum comes alive with flamenco dancing and concerts. Tapas stalls and attractions for kids add to the fun.

JULY

Grec Festival *(Jun–Jul)*. Performers from Catalonia and around the world flock to Barcelona to delight crowds in a six-week soirée.

Cantada d'Havaneres *(1st Sun)*. Singers belt out *havaneres* (habaneras), fuelled by *cremat* (coffee and rum); see the best at Calella de Palafrugell.

△ **Santa Cristina** *(24 Jul)*. The people of Lloret de Mar honour their patron saint.

AUGUST

Porta Ferrada *(Jul–Aug)*. The Costa Brava village of Sant Feliu de Guíxols becomes a centre of the arts.

△ **Circuit Festival** *(early–mid Aug)*. Thousands storm the beaches of Barcelona for this huge LGBT+ party.

Aquelarre de Cervera *(last weekend)*. Be enchanted as witches and the Mascle Cabró (a satyr) take over the town of Cervera.

NOVEMBER

△ **Tots Sants** *(1 Nov)*. The streets fill with the scent of roasted chestnuts and baked sweet potato, as All Saints' Eve dawns. The next day, Dia dels Difunts (All Souls' Day), people visit loved ones' graves.

Nice One Barcelona *(end Nov)*. Gaming nerds, from across the country flex their controller thumbs over three days of Spanish video game industry reveals, forums and launches.

DECEMBER

△ **Fira de Santa Llúcia** *(late Nov–23 Dec)*. Barcelona's oldest Christmas market sees hundreds of stalls set up around Catedral de Barcelona selling handmade gifts.

Fira de l'Avet d'Espinelves *(1st two weeks)*. Espinelves throngs with gift-hunters in the busy Christmas market, full of artisan handicraft and food stalls.

Reveillón *(31 Dec)*. All over Spain on Reveillón (New Year's Eve) people try to eat 12 grapes – one between each chime of the midnight bell.

SPAIN
IN THE ELEVENTH GEN
(after the fall of the Omay
Kingdom of Sancho the Great, divide
on his death in 1035
The Frankish territories   1

A BRIEF
HISTORY

First united under the House of Barcelona, Catalonia has a distinct culture and language thanks to frequent spells of autonomy. Its history is a long tug-of-war between independence and Spanish rule that continues to this day.

Early Catalonia

First inhabited around 8000 BC by cave-painting hunter-gatherers, Catalonia was more permanently settled by the Laeitani and Iberians around 1000 BC. Greek and Cathaginian trading ports, established around 550 BC, were absorbed by the Romans, who arrived at Empúries in 218 BC. They repressed the Iberians and established Tarraco (Tarragona) as their capital.

Visigoths and Moors

Following the collapse of the Roman Empire, the Visigoths moved their base from Toulouse in France to Spain, where they stayed

230 BC
___
Barcelona was founded by Hamilcar Barca, father of Hannibal.

Timeline of events

2000– 1500 BC
Megalithic monuments are built throughout Catalonia.

AD 531
Visigoths establish themselves in Barcelona after the fall of Rome.

550 BC
Greeks establish a trading settlement at Empúries.

218 BC
Romans arrive at Empúries to take Spain.

717
Moors take control of Catalonia.

until the Moors stormed Spain's southern shores in 711. Moving north with impressive speed, the Moors captured Barcelona six years later but their control was short-lived. In the early 9th century Charlemagne reclaimed Barcelona and established the Marca Hispanica, a buffer state to separate Moorish al-Andalus to the south from his own northern kingdom. It was put under the control of local lords and a nascent Catalan nation began to emerge.

Consolidation and Expansion

In 878, Guifré el Pilós (Wilfred the Hairy), the first count of Barcelona, brought the Catalan counties of Barcelona, Cerdanya, Conflent, Osona, Urgell and Girona under his control, and established hereditary rule. Catalonia began to assert more independence and towards the end of the 11th century it established the first constitutional government in Europe with a bill of rights. The region's boundaries pushed south past Tarragona, and united with Aragon, to the north, in 1137. Under the long reign of Jaume I the Conqueror (Jaime I, in Castilian) there was an explosion of Catalan prosperity and maritime expansion. He established the Corts (Calatan Parliament), and promoted Catalan language and literature.

1 Map of the Iberian Peninsula in the 11th century, after the fall of the Moorish caliphate.

2 Finely tiled Roman mosaic of Mnemosyne, mother of the Muses, in Tarragona.

3 Visigothic writing once used on the Iberian Peninsula, set in stone.

4 The conquest of the island of Majorca, under Jaume I of Aragon.

801

Moors are driven out of Catalonia by Charlemagne, who establishes the Marca Hispanica.

878

Guifré el Pilós (Wilfred the Hairy) consolidates the eastern Pyrenees and gains autonomy.

1060

The constitution, the Usatges, is drawn; the word "Catalan" is first recorded.

1137

Barcelona unites with neighbouring Aragon by royal marriage.

1300s

The Corts (Catalan Parliament) is established.

The Catholic Monarchs

Spain was united in 1469 when Fernando II of Catalonia-Aragon married Isabel of Castile, a region which by then had absorbed the rest of northern Spain. In 1492, they reclaimed Granada, the last Muslim-controlled area of the peninsula. Then, in a fever of righteousness, they also drove out the Jewish population. This had a disastrous effect on the economy of Barcelona and Girona. That same year explorer Columbus set foot in America, opening up trade routes that promised unprecedented wealth and prosperity for Spain. However, Barcelona was shut out from the economic potential when Seville and Cádiz were awarded a monopoly over trade with the Americas. As a result of this economic delimitation, Barcelona went into a period of decline and the seeds were sown for centuries of tensions between Catalonia and Castile.

War of Spanish Succession

During the Thirty Years' War, Catalonia eventually allied itself with France rather than Spain, so heightening tensions between Spain and the Catalan state. In the end, Spain's

CATALAN ROMANESQUE

From the 11th century the thick stone and striking decoration of Romanesque architecture flourished in the region, especially in a proliferation of small, beautiful churches in the narrow Vall de Boí. The most characteristic feature is the tall, square belfry (as seen at Sant Climent de Taüll), featuring high, columned windows and radiating chapels.

Timeline of events

1469

Fernando II of Catalonia-Aragon marries Isabel of Castile, uniting Spain under one ruling house.

1492

Columbus lands in the Americas; Barcelona is barred from trade with the Americas.

1494

Supreme Council of Aragon brings Catalonia under Castilian control.

1659

The end of the Thirty Years' War sees the redrawing of the border with France; Roussillon cedes to France.

Felipe IV laid siege to and defeated the region. A second confrontation with Madrid arose during the War of Spanish Succession, when Barcelona allied with England to back the Habsburgs, who eventually lost the Spanish crown to the Bourbons. Following this defeat, Barcelona fell to Felipe V's forces on 11 September 1714. This marked a turning point for Catalonia as Felipe proceeded to annul Catalan independence and privilege. The Catalan language was banned, Catalonia's universities were closed and Felipe built a citadel to keep an eye on the population.

The Catalan Renaixença

Catalonia's fortunes changed once more as Barcelona became the first city in Spain to industrialize in the 1800s. Immigrant workers arrived and the population grew rapidly, eventually bursting out of its medieval city walls. Industrialization led to wealth and prosperity, which inspired the *Renaixença*, a renaissance of the Catalan culture that had been suppressed for over a hundred years. As well as traditional customs and a return to the Catalan language, Catalan art and literature flourished.

1 Isabel of Castille and Fernando of Catalonia-Aragon greeted by the explorer Christopher Columbus.

2 Drawing of the siege of Barcelona by the forces of the Spanish King Felipe V (1714).

3 Engraving of the War of Spanish Succession (1701–1714).

4 Painting of the Sert and Sola Brothers (1882) by Antonio Regalt.

5 *The Working Girl* (1885) by Catalan painter Joan Planella i Rodríguez.

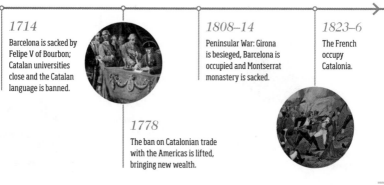

1714

Barcelona is sacked by Felipe V of Bourbon; Catalan universities close and the Catalan language is banned.

1778

The ban on Catalonian trade with the Americas is lifted, bringing new wealth.

1808–14

Peninsular War: Girona is besieged, Barcelona is occupied and Montserrat monastery is sacked.

1823–6

The French occupy Catalonia.

1

2

3

Catalanism and Modernisme

As part of the region's momentum towards autonomy, Felipe V's citadel, a symbol of Madrid's hold on Catalonia, was razed in the 1840s and replaced by a vast public park. In 1887 the first home-rule party, the Lliga de Catalunya, was founded as disputes with the central government continued. Meanwhile, Barcelona continued to expand. The new district of Eixample (Catalan for "expansion") was created on a grid system. Architects such as Antoni Gaudí and Lluís Domènech i Montaner developed a distinctive modernist architectural style to capture the essence of Catalan identity, now considered synonymous with Catalonia.

Civil War and the Franco Era

As Catalonia's re-emerging national identity inspired calls for full independence, momentum was stopped in its tracks by the Spanish Civil War. All of Spain was ravaged from 1936 until 1939. Catalonia was bombed by German aircraft and Italian warships, who had sided with Francisco Franco's Nationalist cause. After the nationalist victory, Franco installed himself as dictator of

↑ An election official carrying a polling box at the 2017 referendum

Timeline of events

1849
Spain's first railway links Barcelona and Mataró.

1859
A revival of Jocs Florals's poetry feeds a revival of Catalan culture.

1888
Universal Exhibition, held in Parc de la Ciutadella, showcases the Modernista style.

1936–9
Spanish Civil War. Nationalist victory sees the suppression of Catalan language, culture and identity.

1960s
Package holidays across the Costa Brava create a boom in tourism.

Spain. Engulfed by what the Catalans call the *negre nit* (dark night), Catalonia was stripped of its autonomy, its language outlawed yet again, and any public displays of separatist sympathy were brutally suppressed. Barcelona was left once again short of resources and largely neglected by the government.

Catalonia Today

Despite Franco's oppressive regime, the 1960s brought an economic boom in the form of tourism along the Costa Brava and Costa Daurada. When Franco died in 1975, constitutional democracy was restored to Spain and Catalonia regained a considerable degree of independence. The city was rejuvenated in 1992 for the Olympic Games and later gained further prominence when it hosted the Universal Forum of Culture in 2004. The global economic crisis of the early 2000s hit Catalonia hard and led again to calls for complete separation from Spain. At the independence referendum, held in October 2017 with a turnout of 43 per cent, the "yes" side won with an absolute majority. However, the referendum was suspended by the Constitutional Court of Spain, furthering the political crisis.

1 The flamboyantly tiled Modernista villa El Capricho in Comillas, designed by Antoni Gaudí.

2 The unique rooftop of Gaudí's famous La Pedrera in Barcelona, built between 1906 and 1910.

3 Crowds waiting in the streets to greet General Francisco Franco's troops.

4 The Estelada (Catalan separatist flag) flying at a protest calling for independence.

1979
Partial autonomy is granted to Catalonia.

1986
Spain joins the European Community (now the European Union) and NATO.

2018
Girona-born Joan Roca wins Best Chef awards for the second year in a row.

1975
Franco dies; King Juan Carlos ascends the throne, restoring the Bourbon line.

2015
Political party Junts pel Sí (Together for Yes) wins Catalan regional elections.

EXPERIENCE

Ambling along Barcelona's La Rambla

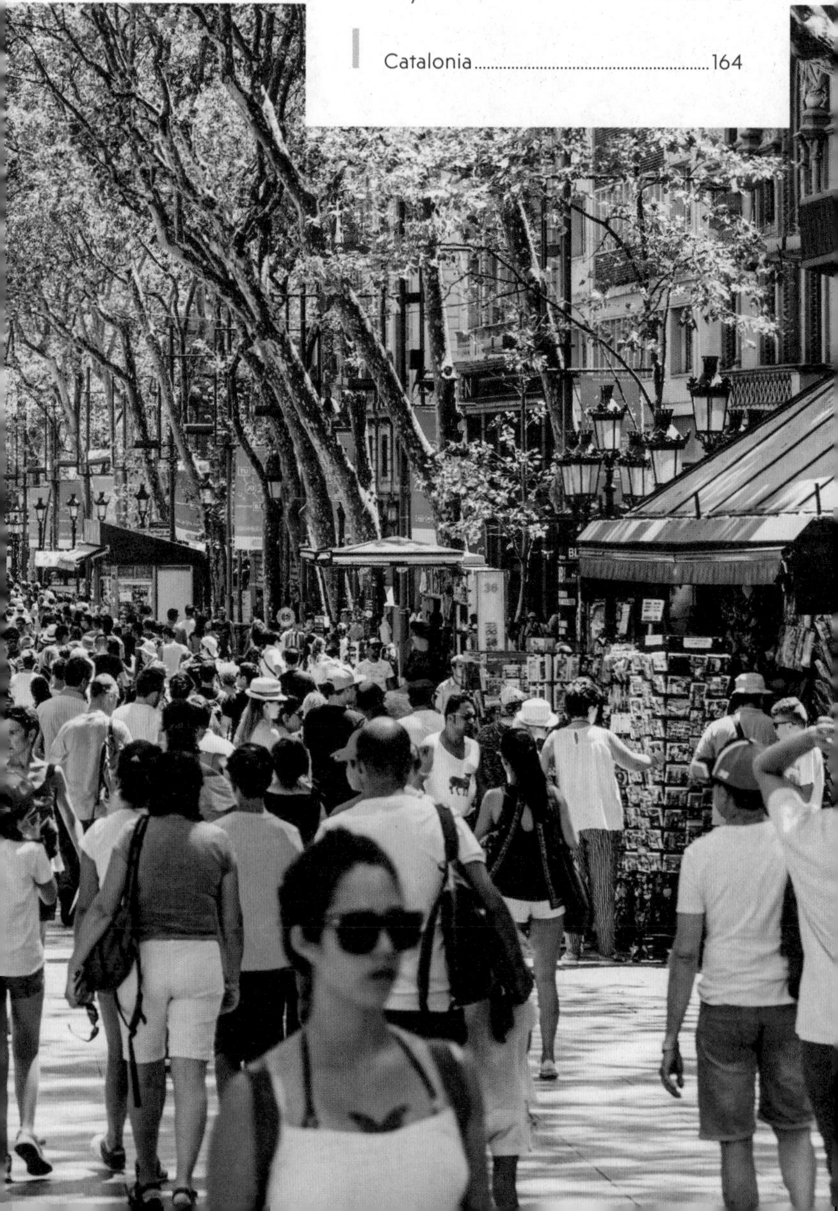

OLD TOWN

Barcelona's Ciutat Vella (Old Town) is where
the city itself came into being. Settled by the
prehistoric Laietani, the area stretching between
the Besòs and Llobregat river deltas was chosen
by the Romans around 15 BC to be the site of their
new *colonia* (town): Barcino. They surrounded the
town with defensive walls, ruins of which can still
be seen today. The Roman forum on the Plaça de
Sant Jaume was replaced by the medieval Palau de
la Generalitat in 1596, the seat of Catalonia's
government, and the Casa de la Ciutat, the city's
town hall. Close by are the Gothic cathedral and
royal palace, where explorer Christopher Columbus
was received by Fernando and Isabel on his return
from the Americas in 1492.

As the medieval town grew wealthy from trade
across the Mediterranean, it expanded out into El
Born and, later, rural El Raval. In the 18th century,
Barceloneta was developed into a fishing quarter.
The medieval walls surrounded the city until the
mid-19th century, when they were torn down for
an urban expansion project which saw the creation
of neighbouring Eixample.

Today, the Old Town remains the beating heart
of the Catalan capital, particularly its main artery
La Rambla, a magnet for locals and tourists alike,
and one of the most vibrant streets in Europe.

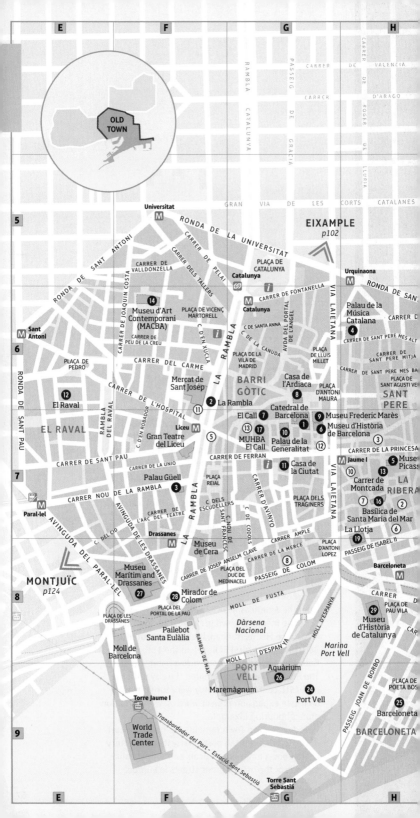

OLD TOWN

Must Sees

1. Catedral de Barcelona
2. La Rambla
3. Palau Güell
4. Palau de la Música Catalana
5. Museu Picasso

Experience More

6. Museu d'Història de Barcelona
7. El Call
8. Casa de l'Ardiaca
9. Museu Frederic Marès
10. Palau de la Generalitat
11. Casa de la Ciutat
12. El Raval
13. Carrer de Montcada
14. Museu d'Art Contemporani (MACBA)
15. Castell dels Tres Dragons
16. Basílica de Santa Maria del Mar
17. MUHBA El Call
18. Parc de la Ciutadella
19. La Llotja
20. El Born Centre de Cultura i Memòria
21. Arc de Triomf
22. Museu de la Xocolata
23. Port Olímpic
24. Port Vell
25. Barceloneta
26. Aquàrium
27. Museu Marítim and Drassanes
28. Mirador de Colom
29. Museu d'Història de Catalunya

Eat

1. Elsa y Fred
2. Cal Pep
3. Bar del Pla
4. Ale&Hop

Drink

5. Cafè de l'Òpera
6. Paradiso
7. La Vinya del Senyor

Stay

8. The Serras Hotel Barcelona
9. Chic & Basic Born
10. Banys Orientals

Shop

11. Escribà
12. Cereria Subirà
13. Artesania Catalunya

CATEDRAL DE BARCELONA

📍 G7 🏛 Plaça de la Seu ⏰ 8:30am–7:30pm daily; Sacristy Museum: 9am–7pm daily Ⓜ Jaume I 🚌 17, 19, 45
🌐 catedralbcn.org

With its intricate façade and inviting interior, Barcelona Cathedral is a beguiling sight. Treading beneath the nave's soaring vaulting, you may feel as if you are stepping back in time.

One of the city's few churches spared from destruction in the Civil War, this compact Gothic cathedral was begun in 1298 under Jaime (Jaume) II on the foundations of a site dating back to Visigothic times, but was not finished until the late 19th century. This interruption has lent Barcelona Cathedral a distinct look compared to the rest of the Barri Gòtic. The cathedral is dedicated to St Eulàlia, the city's patron saint, whose white marble sarcophagus is located in the crypt. Take your time to explore the exceptional interior, as well as the lofty roof terrace and shady cloisters. Visit before 12:45pm or after 5:15pm to skip the entry fee, though a ticket is always required for access to the terrace and choir stalls.

Twin octagonal bell towers, dating from 1386 to 1393

The Catalan-style Gothic interior, with a single wide nave that has 28 side chapels

Beautifully carved choir stalls, which date from the 15th century

The Capella del Santíssim Sagrament

Timeline

877
△ St Eulàlia's remains brought here from Santa Maria del Mar

1046–58
△ Romanesque cathedral built under Ramon Berenguer I

1493
△ Six indigenous Caribbeans, brought from the Americas by Christopher Columbus, are baptized in the cathedral

1889
Main façade completed, based on plans dating from 1408 by architect Charles Galters

The crypt, where St Eulàlia's tomb is found

① The cathedral's central spire was finally completed in 1913.

② The shady Gothic cloisters are especially popular with visitors.

③ The cathedral's crypt is home to the alabaster sarcophagus of St Eulàlia.

The Capella de Sant Benet, a chapel dedicated to the founder of the Benedictine Order and patron saint of Europe, is home to a magnificent altarpiece

← *The distinctive Barcelona Cathedral, set in the city's Old Town*

Porta de Santa Eulàlia, the entrance to the cloisters

Cloisters, with a fountain decorated with a statue of St George

The Sacristy Museum, which houses a small treasury

Capella de Santa Llúcia

Did You Know?

Thirteen geese live in the cloister, representing St Eulàlia's age at her martyrdom.

2 🍴 ☕ 🛍

LA RAMBLA

⊠F6 🚇Drassanes, Liceu, Catalunya 🚃Catalunya

The historic avenue of La Rambla splits the Old Town in half as it stretches from Plaça de Catalunya to Port Vell. Newsstands, flower stalls, tarot readers, musicians and mime artists line the wide, tree-shaded central walkway around the clock, but La Rambla is particularly frenetic in the evenings and at weekends.

The name of this long avenue, known as Les Rambles in Catalan, comes from the Arabic *ramla*, meaning "the dried-up bed of a seasonal river". The 13th-century city wall followed the left bank of such a river that flowed from the Collserola hills to the sea. Convents, monasteries and the university were built on the opposite bank in the 16th century. As time passed, the riverbed was filled in and those buildings demolished, but they are remembered in the names of the five consecutive Rambles that make up the great avenue.

The first of these, Rambla de Canaletes, is named after an extravagant fountain; and Rambla dels Estudis after a university established here in the 16th century. Along the latter, you'll find the Palau Moja. Pop inside the Baroque first-floor salon to learn more about Catalan culture. Next comes Rambla de Sant Josep, where a monastery dedicated to the saint was demolished to make room for the market better known as "La Boqueria" – the place where *boc* (goat) is sold. Don't miss the Palau de le Virreina, which hosts free exhibitions. Rambla dels Caputxins and Rambla de Santa Mònica also recall a long-gone monastery and convent.

→

A living statue, dressed as a golden monster, striking a pose on La Rambla

EAT

Mercat de Sant Josep
"La Boqueria" is Barcelona's most colourful food market. Seek out Bar Quiosc Modern for its seafood.

🏠 Plaça de la Boqueria
🕐 Sun 🌐 boqueria. barcelona

€€€

Rocambolesc
The ice cream at this kiosk is served up by the Roca brothers, who are regularly voted the best chefs in the world.

🏠 La Rambla 51-59
🌐 rocambolesc.com

€€€

↑ Punters sampling dishes at the busy food stalls inside La Boqueria

Did You Know?

The poet Lorca said La Rambla was "the only street in the world that I wish would never end".

↑ Tree-lined La Rambla snaking through the heart of Barcelona towards distant hills

3 ⊘ ⊘ ⊞

PALAU GÜELL

⦿F7 **◯Nou de la Rambla 3-5** **◻Liceu** **◷Apr-Oct: 10am-8pm Tue-Sun; Nov-Mar: 10am-5:30pm Tue-Sun** **◷1, 6 & 19-25 Jan, 25 & 26 Dec** **ⓦpalauguell.cat**

Half-hidden on a narrow side street off La Rambla, Antoni Gaudí's first major building in Barcelona quickly established his international reputation for outstanding, original architecture. It was built in 1889 for the industrialist Eusebi Güell, who would go on to become Gaudí's lifelong patron.

Unusually for Gaudí, this austere, grey house is characterized by straight horizontal and vertical lines. All that hints at his future style are the parabolic arched doorways; the spire-like chimneys behind the parapet on the roof; and the spiral cobbled ramp that swoops down to the basement, where large stone arches reach from torch-shaped columns to support the roof.

Güell made it known that there would be no limit to the budget at Gaudí's disposal, and Gaudí took him at his word, using only the best materials and craftsmen. The most notable feature of the house is its very high central room on the main floor. Something between a sitting room and a covered court-yard, this central room rises three floors and is spanned by a cupola. The other rooms are grouped around it.

> **💬 INSIDER TIP**
> **Les Nits del Palau Güell**
>
> On Thursday nights in summer, the Palau Güell transforms into a per-formance space for a diverse programme of musicians. Concertgoers can go up to the rooftop for cava and nibbles before showtime.

Upper galleries are richly decorated with carved wood and cofferwork

→
Cut-away illustration of Antoni Gaudí's rather austere Palau Güell

Dramatic cupola

▽ A dramatic three-storey cupola covering the central salon, inspired by Islamic architecture, gives the illusion of stars.

Spiral Ramp

The spiral carriage ramp is an early sign of Gaudí's predilection for curved lines.

Highlights

Decorated Chimneys

▲ The colourful glazed tiles that decorate the chimneys became one of the trademarks of Gaudí's later work.

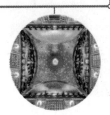

Parabolic Arches

Parabolic arches, used extensively by Gaudí, beginning in the Palau Güell, show his interest in Gothic architecture.

A dramatic
cupola

Elaborate
wrought-iron lamps
light the grand hall

Chimneys bizarrely decorated
with colourful ceramic tiles

A shield alludes
to the Catalan
coat of arms

Organic forms inspired
the wrought iron around
the gates to the palace

The spiral
carriage
ramp

Parabolic
arches

→

The rich wrought-iron
main doors leading into
the main hall

Did You Know?

The Palau's concert hall is the only one in Europe to be lit by natural light.

4 ⚒ 🏛

PALAU DE LA MÚSICA CATALANA

📍H6 🏛Carrer Palau de la Música 4-6 🚇Urquinaona ⏰10am-3:30pm daily; Easter & Jul 10am-6pm daily; Aug 9am-6pm daily; and for concerts 🌐palaumusica.cat

This is a true monument to music, a Modernista celebration of tilework, sculpture and stained glass. Designed by Lluís Domènech i Montaner, it was completed in 1908. Its red-brick façade is elaborate, but it's the main auditorium that is truly inspiring.

The Palace of Catalan Music was built for the Orfeó Català in 1891, a choral society that played an important role in the Catalan cultural resistance known as the "Renaixença". The building's façade is richly decorated with colourful murals, as well as an enormous sculptural group depicting "Catalan Song" and Sant Jordi, the Catalan patron saint.

Inside, the main auditorium is one of the most beautiful in the world, lit by an inverted dome of stained glass portraying angelic choristers. Sculptures of Wagner and Clavé adorn the proscenium arch above the stage, which features a charming group of dancing muses. An underground concert hall and an outdoor square for summer concerts were later added, consolidating the Palau's reputation as Barcelona's most loved music venue.

📷 PICTURE PERFECT
On the Balcony

Book a tour in advance to gain access to the site's balcony. It's the ideal spot to snap the gorgeous stained-glass skylight framed by the auditorium. The colourful tiled pillars are also worth a close-up shot.

THE SARDANA

Catalonia's national dance is more complicated than it appears. The success of the Sardana depends on all of the dancers accurately counting the complicated short- and long-step skips and jumps, which accounts for their serious faces. Music is provided by a *cobla*, an 11-person band consisting of a leader playing a three-holed flute *(flabiol)* and a little drum *(tambor)*, five woodwind players and five brass players. When the music starts, dancers join hands and form circles. The Sardana is performed at most local fiestas and the Palau de la Música Catalana stages performances sometimes.

↑ Interior of the Palau's sublime concert hall, beneath its inverted stained-glass dome

↑ American jazz singer Madeleine Peyrou performing in the Palau

→ The ornate, pillared façade of the Palau, lit up at dusk

← A scuplture of the composer Lluís Millet standing at the Palau

Visitors wandering ↑ through stone archways inside the Museu Picasso

MUSEU PICASSO

📍H7 🏛Carrer de Montcada 15-23 🚇Jaume I 🕐Jan-Oct: 10am-5pm Mon, 9am-8:30pm Tue-Sun (to 9:30pm Thu); Nov & Dec: 9am-7pm Tue-Sun (to 9:30pm Thu) 🌐museupicasso.bcn.cat

One of Barcelona's most popular attractions, the Picasso Museum is housed in five adjoining medieval palaces: Berenguer d'Aguilar, Baró de Castellet, Meca, Mauri and Finestres. The collection focuses largely on Picasso's early work, showing the development of the young painter and the influence of the city that was his home for many years.

The core of the Picasso Museum's collection is a large donation made in 1963 by the artist's secretary and great friend, Jaume Sabartés. Given that Picasso had publicly sworn that he wouldn't set foot in Spain while Franco lived, it was known as the Sabartés Collection for many years (as a museum using the artist's own name would have been met with censorship). Following Sabartés' death in 1968, Picasso himself donated further paintings, including early examples. These were later complemented by graphic works, left in his will, and 141 ceramic pieces given by his widow, Jacqueline.

The setting of the museum itself makes for a unique experience. Visitors are able to wander through stone archways, into pretty courtyards and up well-preserved staircases as they take in the artworks.

The strength of the 4,200-piece collection, which includes sketches, paintings, sculptures and ceramics, is Picasso's early works. These show how, even at the ages of 15 and 16, he had prodigious talent, while the haunting paintings of his Blue Period evoke the misery and hopelessness of beggars and prostitutes he encountered on Barcelona's streets. The highlight of the museum's collection, however, is Picasso's extraordinary suite of 58 paintings, which he created in response to Velázquez's masterpiece, *Las Meninas* (1656).

← A portrait of Picasso in his later years

↑ One of the paintings in Picasso's *Las Meninas* series (1957)

PABLO PICASSO IN BARCELONA

Picasso (1881-1973) was born in Málaga and was almost 14 when he came to Barcelona. He enrolled in the city's art academy and was a precocious talent among his contemporaries. Amid the prostitutes of Carrer d'Avinyó, Picasso found inspiration for his *Les Demoiselles d'Avignon* (1906-7). He left Barcelona for Paris in his early twenties and returned several times, but after the Civil War his opposition to Franco kept him in France.

EXPERIENCE MORE

6

Museu d'Història de Barcelona

☉ G7 ⚑ Plaça del Rei
⬚ Jaume I ☉ 10am-7pm
Tue-Sat, 10am-8pm Sun
⬚ 1 Jan, 1 May, 24 Jun, 25 Dec
⬚ museuhistoria.bcn.cat

A building of great historical importance, the Palau Reial (Royal Palace) is an apt location for Barcelona's multi-sited Museu d'Història. It was the residence of the counts of Barcelona from its foundation in the 13th century. It was here that Isabel and Fernando received explorer Christopher Columbus after his return from the Americas, in the 14th-century Gothic Saló del Tinell, a vast room with arches spanning 17 m (56 ft). This room is also the site of the Holy Inquisition, the proponents of which believed the walls would move if lies were told. Built into the Roman city wall is the royal chapel, the Capella de Santa Àgata, with a painted wood ceiling and an altarpiece by Jaume Huguet. Stairs on the right of the altar

lead to the 16th-century tower of Martí the Humanist (who reigned from 1396 to 1410), the last ruler of the 500-year dynasty of the count-kings of Barcelona. The tower is not open to visitors.

The museum's highlight lies below ground. Entire streets of old Barcino (Roman Barcelona) are accessible via a lift and walkways suspended over the ruins. The site was discovered when the Casa Clariana-Padellàs, the Gothic building from which you enter, was moved here, stone by stone, in 1931, as depicted in a photo of the original dig. The water systems, homes with mosaic floors and even the old forum now make up the most extensive subterranean Roman ruins in the world.

7

El Call

☉ G7 ⬚ Jaume I, Liceu

Named for the Hebrew word *kahal*, meaning community or congregation, El Call remains the centre of Jewish life in

Barcelona. Ghettoized in 1243 following a wave of anti-Semitic violence, it had been abandoned by its Jewish community long before the expulsion of the Jews in 1424 by Catholic Isabel and Fernando.

Today, nestled in the Old Town's Barri Gòtic, the lively neighbourhood once again

---

BARCELONA'S EARLY JEWISH COMMUNITY

First documented in Barcelona in 889, evidence suggests the first synagogue was founded in the 5th century. The city's Jewish community grew to 15 per cent of the city's population by the 14th century, providing doctors and the first seat of learning. Chronic violent anti-Semitism led to the Jews being consigned to El Call. The ghetto was abandoned in 1401, 91 years before Judaism was fully outlawed in Spain.

Locals relaxing in the square outside the Museu d'Història de Barcelona

flourishes, with modern synagogues and kosher shops, while remnants of the medieval Jewish character of these narrow streets remain. Descend into the basement of the Café Caelum to see ancient Jewish baths. Around the corner, in the wall at No 5 Carrer de Marlet, a 14th-century Hebrew tablet reads: "Holy Foundation of Rabbi Samuel Hassardi. His soul will rest in Heaven." The 5th-century remains of the city's oldest synagogue, lost as a place of worship in the 15th century, was restored and reopened for special events in 2002.

8

Casa de l'Ardiaca

🅖 G6 🏠 Carrer de Santa Llúcia 1 📞 93 256 22 55 🚇 Jaume I 🕐 9am-8:45pm Mon-Fri, 10am-8pm Sat

Standing beside what was originally the Bishop's Gate in the city's Roman wall is the

Archdeacon's House. It was first built in the 12th century, but in its present form it dates from around 1500, when it was remodelled, including the addition of a colonnade. In 1870, the colonnade was further extended to form the Flamboyant Gothic patio around a fountain. Modernista architect Domènech i Montaner added the fanciful marble mailbox, carved with three swallows and a tortoise, beside the Renaissance portal. Upstairs is the Arxiu Històric de la Ciutat (City Archives).

---

9 🏷️

Museu Frederic Marès

🅖 G7 🏠 Plaça de Sant Iu 5 🚇 Jaume I 🕐 10am-7pm Tue-Sat, 11am-8pm Sun & pub hols 🚫 1 Jan, 1 May, 24 Jun, 25 Dec 🌐 museu mares.bcn.cat

The sculptor Frederic Marès i Deulovol (1893–1991) was also a traveller and collector, and this

Stone arches and *(inset)* exhibits at the Museu Frederic Marès ↓

museum is a monument to his eclectic taste. As part of the Royal Palace, it was occupied by 13th-century bishops, 14th-century counts of Barcelona, 15th-century judges and 18th-century nuns, who lived here until they were expelled in 1936. Marès, who had a small apartment in the building, opened this museum in 1948. It contains a fascinating collection of works, including some outstanding examples of Romanesque and Gothic religious art. In the crypt and on the ground floor are stone sculptures and two complete Romanesque portals. The first floor has Renaissance and Baroque sculpture. Exhibits on the second and third floors are more varied, with pieces ranging from children's toys, clocks and costumes to antique cameras, smoking pipes and postcards.

↑ The richly decorated ceiling of the Sant Jordi chapel in the Palau de la Generalitat

10

Palau de la Generalitat

G7 **Plaça de Sant Jaume 4** **Jaume I** **2nd & 4th Sat & Sun of month Sep-Jul: 10:30am-1:30pm by appt only; passport needed for entry** **president.cat**

Since 1403, the Generalitat has been the seat of the Catalonian government. The Catalan president has offices here and in the next door Casa dels Canonges. The *casa* (house) and the Generalitat are connected across Carrer del Bisbe by a 1928 bridge modelled on the Bridge of Sighs in Venice.

A statue of Sant Jordi (St George) – the patron saint of Catalonia – and the Dragon stand guard above the entrance. The late Catalan Gothic courtyard and the fine Gothic chapel of Sant Jordi are both by Marc Safont, while the Italianate Saló de Sant Jordi is by Pere Blai. The Palau

holds three open days a year: 23 April, and 11 and 24 September.

At the back, above street level, lies the Pati dels Tarongers (Orange Tree Courtyard) by master builder Pau Mateu, which has a bell tower built by Pere Ferrer in 1568.

11

Casa de la Ciutat

G7 **Plaça de Sant Jaume 1** **93 402 70 00** **Jaume I, Liceu** **10am-2pm Sun; 23 Apr and 30 May: 10am-8pm**

The magnificent 14th-century *ajuntament* (city hall) faces the Palau de la Generalitat. Flanking the entrance are

statues of Jaume I, who granted the city rights to elect councillors in 1249, and Joan Fiveller, who levied taxes on court members in the 1500s. Inside is the council chamber, the 14th-century Saló de Cent, built for the city's 100 councillors. The first-floor Saló de les Cròniques was commissioned for the 1929 International Exhibition and decorated by Josep Maria Sert with murals of events in Catalan history.

12

El Raval

E6 **Catalunya, Liceu**

The district of El Raval lies west of La Rambla *(p72)* and includes the area near the port, once known as Barri Xinès (Chinese Quarter).

From the 14th century, the city hospital was located in Carrer de l'Hospital, which still has several herbal and medicinal shops today. Gaudí *(p84)* was brought here after being fatally hit by a tram in 1926. The buildings now house the Biblioteca de Catalunya (Catalonian Library), but you can visit the elegantly restored former dissecting room.

Towards the port on Carrer Nou de la Rambla is Gaudí's Palau Güell *(p74)*. At the end

→ Barcelona's Museu d'Art Contemporani, aglow with colourful lights at night

of Carrer Sant Pau is the city's most complete Romanesque church, the 12th-century Sant Pau del Camp, with a charming cloister featuring exquisitely carved capitals.

🔟 Carrer de Montcada

◉ H7 🚇 Jaume I

The most authentic medieval street in the city, this narrow lane is overshadowed by gargoyles and roofs that almost touch overhead. The Gothic palaces that line it date back to Catalonia's expansion in the 13th century. Almost all of the buildings were modified over the years, particularly during the 17th century. Only Casa Cervelló-Guidice at No 25 retains its original façade.

> 🔍 **HIDDEN GEM**
> ### Casa de la Seda
>
> A ten-minute walk from Carrer de Montcada is the Casa de la Seda or "House of Silk", the former headquarters of the silkmakers' guild. Visit to take a tour through sumptuously decorated rooms *(www.casadelaseda.com)*.

---

14 Museu d'Art Contemporani (MACBA)

◉ F6 ☉ Plaça dels Ángels 1 🚇 Universitat, Catalunya
⏱ 25 Sep-24 Jun: 11am-7:30pm Mon & Wed-Fri, 10am-8pm Sat, 10am-3pm Sun; 25 Jun-24 Sep: 10am-7:30pm Mon & Wed-Fri, 10am-8pm Sat, 10am-3pm Sun 🚫 1 Jan, 25 Dec
🌐 macba.cat

This glass-fronted building was designed by the renowned American architect Richard Meier. Its light, airy galleries serve as the city's contemporary art mecca. The permanent collection of mainly Spanish painting and sculpture from the 1950s onwards is complemented by temporary exhibitions by international artists, among them South African photo-journalist David Goldblatt.

Next to the MACBA is the **Centre de Cultura Contemporània de Barcelona** (CCCB), a lively arts centre.

Centre de Cultura Contemporània de Barcelona
🚻 ☉ Montalegre 5 ⏱ 11am-8pm Tue-Sun 🌐 cccb.org

DRINK

Cafè de l'Òpera

Strategically positioned across from the opera house, this bastion of faded elegance is one spot worth stopping at.

◉ F7 ☉ La Rambla 74 🌐 cafeoperabcn.com

Paradiso

Accessed through the refrigerator door of a pastrami bar, this hidden speakeasy has inspired cocktails.

◉ H7 ☉ Carrer Rera Palau 4 🌐 paradiso.cat

La Vinya del Senyor

A tiny wine bar with a sprawling terrace, this is a relaxing pit stop in the heart of El Born.

◉ H7 ☉ Plaça de Santa María 5 📞 93 310 3379

GAUDÍ'S CITY

Barcelona bears the indelible mark of Catalonia's most famous son, Antoni Gaudí i Cornet, who transformed the city's skyline into an architectural masterpiece. Drawing on Persian and Japanese arts, Mudéjar architecture and the natural world, Gaudí reinvented the already adventurous art and architectural style known as Catalan Modernisme. A highly dexterous architect, Gaudí designed or collaborated on designs in almost every known medium. He combined bare, undecorated materials – wood, rough-hewn stone, rubble and brickwork – with meticulous craftwork in wrought iron, stained glass and elaborate mosaics. Every Gaudí creation is unique, but they are united by their skill and romanticism.

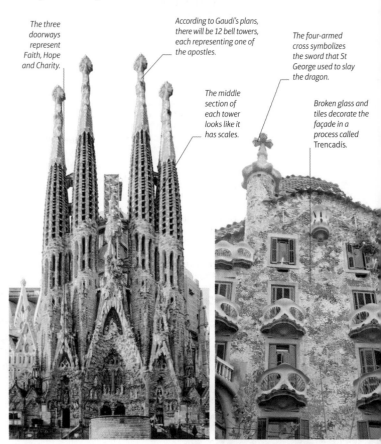

The three doorways represent Faith, Hope and Charity.

According to Gaudí's plans, there will be 12 bell towers, each representing one of the apostles.

The four-armed cross symbolizes the sword that St George used to slay the dragon.

The middle section of each tower looks like it has scales.

Broken glass and tiles decorate the façade in a process called Trencadís.

Gaudí Highlights

Sagrada Família

▲ When Gaudí took over the construction of the Sagrada Família *(p106)* in 1883, it became his lifelong obsession. An extreme expression of devotion, his soaring interior and the Nativity façade reference both biblical events and the natural world. Although he never lived to see its completion, it is still built to his vision.

Casa Batlló

▲ Industrialist Josep Batlló gave Gaudí complete creative freedom to reform this late-19th-century house. Completed in 1906, Casa Batlló *(p112)* is an evocation of artistic joy. The façade acted as an exuberant and marine-inspired canvas, while the roof ripples like a dragon in flight. Inside, light pours in through effervescent stained glass, while the central patio ensures natural light reaches every room.

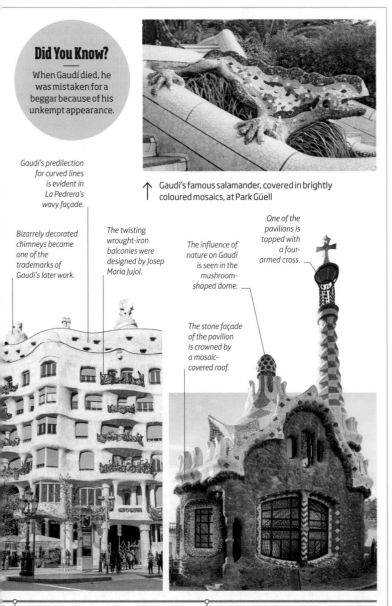

Gaudí's predilection for curved lines is evident in La Pedrera's wavy façade.

↑ Gaudí's famous salamander, covered in brightly coloured mosaics, at Park Güell

Bizarrely decorated chimneys became one of the trademarks of Gaudí's later work.

The twisting wrought-iron balconies were designed by Josep Maria Jujol.

The influence of nature on Gaudí is seen in the mushroom-shaped dome.

One of the pavilions is topped with a four-armed cross.

The stone façade of the pavilion is crowned by a mosaic-covered roof.

La Pedrera

△ The last private residence to be designed by Gaudí, rough-hewn La Pedrera *(p114)* raised eyebrows in its time due to its undulating stone façade, abstract roof sculptures and opera-mask-like balconies. The entrance doors, designed to facilitate both people and vehicles, are made up of smaller panes of glass in irregular shapes, based on animals and plants, with larger, more luminous pieces at the top.

Park Güell

△ Belonging to Gaudí's naturalist phase, Park Güell *(p144)* is emblematic of the architect's fanciful style. The stone-built pavilions, with their brightly tiled gingerbread roofs, are like something from a fairy-tale. One of these lodges was designed to be the Casa del Guarda (Caretaker's House). Initially conceived to be a garden city for Barcelona's wealthy families, only two plots were purchased.

SHOP

Escribà

Find cakes, chocolates and other Wonka-esque delights at this this decades-old patisserie.

📍 F6 🏠 La Rambla 83 Ⓦ escriba.es

Cereria Subirà

Pick up beautiful handmade wax creations at this lovely candlemaker's.

📍 G7 🏠 Baixada de la Llibreteria 7 Ⓦ cereriasubira.cat

Artesania Catalunya

Come for the best artisanal products of the region.

📍 G7 🏠 Carrer des Banys Nous 11 Ⓦ bcncrafts.com

15

Castell dels Tres Dragons

📍 J7 🏠 Passeig de Picasso 📞 93 256 22 00 🚇 Arc de Triomf, Jaume I 🔒 To the public

At the entrance to the Parc de la Ciutadella (*p88*) is the fortress-like Castell dels Tres Dragons (Castle of the Three Dragons), probably named after a play by Serafí Pitarra (Frederic Soler). A classic example of Catalonia's Modernista architecture, this crenellated brick edifice was built by Lluís Domènech i Montaner for the 1888 Universal Exhibition. He later used the building as a work-shop for Modernista design, and it became a focus of the movement. Shortly after-wards it housed the History Museum and was later the home of the Biology Museum. The building now serves as a laboratory of the Science Museum and is open only to researchers.

---

16 Ⓜ

Basílica de Santa Maria del Mar

📍 H7 🏠 Pl Sta Maria 1 🚇 Jaume I 🕐 9am-1pm & 5-8:30pm Mon-Sat, 10am-2pm & 5-8pm Sun Ⓦ santa mariadelmarbarcelona.org

This beautiful building, the name of which translates as Our Lady of the Sea, is the city's favourite church. It has superb acoustics for concerts and is the only example of a church entirely in the Catalan Gothic style. Completed in 1383 the basilica took just 55 years to build, with money donated by local merchants and shipbuilders. This speed – unrivalled in the Middle Ages – gave it a unity of style both inside and out. The west front features a 15th-century rose window of the Coronation of the Virgin. More stained glass from the 15th to the 18th centuries lights the

Crenellated Castell dels Tres Dragons rising from the trees ↑

The spectacular Basílica de Santa Maria del Mar ↑

wide nave and high aisles. Though the choir stalls, the Baroque altar and furnishings were burned in the Civil War, their simple restoration creates a sense of space. Guided tours of the basilica's roof are available, offering a lovely opportunity to learn about this church's fascinating history as well as the chance to take in incredible views of Barcelona. Alternatively, take a tour of the church at dusk, to explore the space without battling the usual crowds.

MUHBA El Call

📍 G7 🏠 Placeta de Manuel Ribé s/n 🚇 Jaume I, Liceu 🕐 11am-2pm Wed, 11am-7pm Sat & Sun 🌐 museu historia.bcn.cat

One of the many branches of the Museu d'Història de Barcelona (p80), this information centre occupies a modern building over what was once the home of Yusef Bonhiac, a medieval weaver. Its small collection includes artifacts from medieval life in El Call, Barcelona's former Jewish quarter, such as two tombstones inscribed with Hebrew. The touch-screen information panels and exhibitions give an excellent overview of the area and the lives of its inhabitants. The centre also runs walking tours, fascinating lectures on medieval Barcelona, tastings of Catalan-Jewish cuisine and Jewish storytelling sessions.

→

Parc de la Ciutadella's epic
fountain and *(inset)* its
pleasant boating lake

⓲
Parc de la Ciutadella

📍J7 🏠Passeig de Picasso 1
🚇Barceloneta, Ciutadella-
Vila Olímpica 🕐8am-
sunset daily

Colourful parrots take flight
from the tops of palm trees
and orange groves dotted
about this popular park. A
perfect picnic spot, the city's
largest central green space
was once the site of a massive
star-shaped citadel, built for
Felipe V between 1715 and
1720 following a 13-month
siege of Barcelona. The fortress
was intended to house soldiers
to keep law and order, but was
never used for this purpose. It
was converted into a prison

and became notorious during
the Napoleonic occupation,
and, during the 19th-century
liberal repressions, it was
much-hated as a symbol
of centralized power.

In 1878, under General
Prim, whose statue stands in
the middle of the park, the
citadel was pulled down and
the park given to the city to
become, in 1888, the venue
of the Universal Exhibition.
Three buildings survived: the
Governor's Palace, now a
school; the chapel; and the
arsenal, which remains home
to the Catalan parliament.

The park offers more
cultural and leisure activities
than any other in the city,
and is particularly popular
on Sunday afternoons when
people gather to play instruments, dance, relax, head out
onto the boating lake for
a punt or enjoy a visit to the
museum and zoo.

The **Zoo de Barcelona** was
laid out in the 1940s to what
was, for the time, a relatively
enlightened design; although
the enclosures are not large,
the animals are separated by
moats instead of bars.

Some of the zoo's aquatic
creatures will eventually
be moved to a designated
marine zoo; however, plans
are currently on hold due to
budget cuts.

Standing by the zoo's
entrance is a replica of an 1885
sculpture by Catalan artist
Roig i Soler, *The Lady of the
Umbrella*, which has become
a symbol of Barcelona (the
original statue is stored by
the council). The zoo has a
plethora of family-friendly
activities, including electric
cars, a train ride, a face-
painting area and a petting
zoo, ideal for smaller children.

A trove of works by Catalan
sculptors, such as Marès, Arnau,

💬 INSIDER TIP
Laps of the Lake

On a sunny day, there's
nothing nicer than
renting a rowboat, and
heading out on the lake
in the middle of the Parc
de la Ciutadella. It's
especially popular on
Sunday afternoons; go
early to beat the crowds.

Carbonell, Clarà, Llimona, Gargallo, Dunyach and Fuxà, can be found across the park, alongside work by contemporary artists such as Tàpies and Botero.

Along the park's southern boundary is an imposing Neo-Classical building, designed by the architect Antoni Rovira i Trias. Opened in 1882 to house a natural science and archaeological collection, it is currently being renovated as a branch of the Science Museum, and only the library is open to the public while these works continue. Once completed, it will house a permanent exhibition on the history of the natural sciences.

The northeastern corner of the park features a magnificent fountain, a cascading waterfall topped by a chariot rider spurring on a team of horses and flanked by griffins caught in mid-roar. It was designed by architect Josep Fontseré, with the help of Antoni Gaudí, who was himself a young student at the time.

Zoo de Barcelona

📍 Parc de la Ciutadella
🚇 Ciutadella-Vila Olímpica
🕐 Apr–mid-May & Oct: 10am–7pm daily; mid-May–mid-Sep 10am–8pm daily; Nov–Mar: 10am–5:30pm daily 🌐 zoo barcelona.com

19
La Llotja

📍 H7 📍 Carrer del Consolat de Mar 2 🚇 Barceloneta 🔒 To public (except for special events) 🌐 casa llotja.com

La Llotja (meaning commodity exchange) was built in the 1380s as the headquarters of the Consolat de Mar. It was remodelled in Neo-Classical style in 1771 and housed the city's stock exchange until 1994, the original Gothic hall acting as the trading floor.

The upper floors housed the Barcelona School of Fine Arts, attended by the young Picasso and Joan Miró.

←

Tigers prowling their fern-filled enclosure at Barcelona Zoo

20 El Born Centre de Cultura i Memòria

📍H7 📮Plaça Comercial 12 🚇Jaume I, Barceloneta 🕐Mar-Oct: 10am-8pm Tue-Sun; Nov-Feb: 10am-7pm Tue-Sun 🌐elbornculturai memoria.barcelona.cat

This covered market, with its ornate ironwork and crystal roof, was Barcelona's main market until the early 1970s, when it outgrew its location.

While the market was being remodelled, extensive ruins of the 18th-century city were discovered beneath its foundations. These ruins are now the focal point of the El Born cultural centre, set off by talks, exhibitions and screenings.

The street names here hint at the trade in Barcelona's old mercantile hub: Flassaders was where you would go for a woven blanket; Vidrieria was once lit up with glass-blowers' torches. A few of these establishments remain, but they are now significantly outnumbered by chic boutiques.

Much of this area was razed after Barcelona fell to the French-Spanish forces during the War of Succession. This key event is remembered each year on 11 September, with activities focused on a monument dedicated to those who died in 1714, which is located near the market.

21 Arc de Triomf

📍J6 📮Passeig Lluís Companys 🚇Arc de Triomf

The main gateway to the 1888 Universal Exhibition, which filled the Parc de la Ciutadella (*p88*), was designed by Josep Vilaseca i Casanovas. It is built of brick in Mudéjar (Spanish Moorish) style, with sculpted allegories of crafts, industry and business. The frieze by Josep Reynés on the main façade represents the city welcoming foreign visitors. Reliefs on one side symbolize agriculture and industry, and on the other commerce and art. Climb to the viewing terrace at the top of the arch during the 48h Open House Barcelona festival, held at the end of October.

22 Museu de la Xocolata

📍H7 📮Comerç 36 🚇Jaume I, Arc de Triomf 🕐10am-7pm Mon-Sat; 10am-3pm Sun & public hols 🚫1 & 6 Jan, 25 & 26 Dec 🌐museu xocolata.cat

Founded by Barcelona's chocolate- and pastry-makers' union, this museum takes you through the history of one of

The richly decorated Arc de Triomf, a major Barcelona landmark ↑

the most universally loved foods. The chocolatey exhibits cover the discovery of cocoa in South America through to the invention of the first chocolate machine in Barcelona, using old posters, photographs and footage. The real thing is displayed in a homage to the art of the *mona* – a Catalan invention, this was a traditional Easter cake that evolved over centuries into an edible sculpture. Every year, *pastissiers* compete to create finely decorated chocolate versions of landmarks or folk figures with jewels and other materials.

As well as activities for children, the museum hosts workshops for adults. Don't miss the museum's shop, which sells – you guessed it – all manner of delicious chocolatey treats. Have a taste for more? Carrer de Petrixol, 1 km (half a mile) away, is known as "sweet street" for its myriad chocolate shops. Locals flock here to indulge in steaming cups of drinking chocolate.

↑ The picturesque marina at Port Olímpic, bustling with small pleasure boats

23

Port Olímpic

📍 L9 🚇 Ciutadella-Vila Olímpica

A gateway to some of the city's best beaches, Port Olímpic was created out of the old industrial waterfront to host sailing events for the 1992 summer Olympics. The dramatic makeover redefined the city's skyline and laid out 4 km (2 miles) of open promenade and pristine stretches of sand. The marina, also built for the 1992 games, is home to one of the city's most eye-catching symbols – *El Peix*, the emblematic golden fish sculpture by Canadian artist Frank Gehry. The spectacular fish stretches, 56 m (184 ft) long, next to the water and its steel scales glimmer in the sunshine.

📷 PICTURE PERFECT
Pailebot Santa Eulàlia

Bobbing in the water at the palm-lined Moll de la Fusta (Timber Quay) is an elegant three-mast schooner, originally christened *Carmen Flores*. It first set sail from Spain in 1918. In 1997, the Museum Marítim beautifully restored the ship.

On the seafront are twin 44-floor buildings, Spain's second- and third-tallest skyscrapers, one occupied by offices, the other by the Hotel Arts. They stand beside the former Vila Olímpica built to house athletes. Now a residential area, the complex has shops, nightclubs and bars, as well as two levels of restaurants around the waterside, which have made it a popular place to eat out. There is a wide variety of international cuisines on offer, catering to the tastes of the visitors who make use of the berthing facilities here. The breezy outdoor setting attracts office workers at lunchtime and pleasure-seekers in the evenings and at weekends.

After lunching on plates of fresh seafood, take off your shoes and head onto the sand for a stroll along the string of beaches extending in either direction, edged by the palm-fringed promenade. Behind the promenade, the coastal road winds around a palm-filled park that lies beside another three beaches, each divided by rocky breakwaters. Swimming is safe off the gently sloping, sandy strands. For those seeking a more energetic experience, several of the marina's charter firms offer boating excursions, "taster" sailing trips, kayaking and paddle-surfing.

㉔

Port Vell

⑨ G9 ⊗ Barceloneta, Drassanes

Barcelona's marina is located at the foot of La Rambla (p72), just beyond the old customs house. This house was built in 1902 at the Portal de la Pau, the city's former maritime entrance. To the south, the Moll de Barcelona serves as the passenger pier for visiting liners. In front of the customs house, La Rambla is connected to the yacht clubs on the Moll d'Espanya by a swing bridge and a pedestrian jetty, known as La Rambla de Mar. The Moll d'Espanya is home to Barcelona's impressive Aquàrium and a vast shopping and restaurant complex, the Maremagnum.

On the shore, the Moll de la Fusta (Timber Wharf) has striking red structures inspired by the bridge at Arles, in France, painted by Van Gogh in 1888. At the end of the wharf is the colourful *El Cap de Barcelona (Barcelona Head)*, a 20-m- (66-ft-) tall sculpture by renowned Pop artist Roy

Lichtenstein. The attractive Luxury Marina on the other side of the Moll d'Espanya was once lined with warehouses. Today there is only one left: the former General Stores building, which is also the sole building still standing from Barcelona's Old Port. The stores were designed in 1881 by the engineer Maurici Garrán and were originally intended for use as trading depots. They were refurbished in 1992 and today house the Museu d'Història de Catalunya (p97). Superlative views of the port can be seen from the top of Mirador a Colom (p96).

> **⬛ GREAT VIEW**
> **Golondrinas**
>
> Board a *golondrina* (meaning "swallow") – a small double-decker boat – for a sightseeing trip around Port Vell. The tours take 40 to 60 minutes and offer fantastic from-the-sea views of the steep, castle-topped hill of Montjuïc towards the industrial port.

㉕

Barceloneta

⑨ H9 ⊗ Barceloneta

Barcelona's fishing "village", which lies on a triangular tongue of land jutting into the sea just below the city centre, is renowned for its little restaurants and cafés, and its friendly, intimate air. Its beach is also the closest to the city centre and is well equipped with lifeguards, wheelchair access, showers and play areas for children.

The area was designed in 1753 by the architect and military engineer Juan Martín Cermeño to rehouse people made homeless by the construction, just inland, of the Ciutadella fortress (p88). Laid out in an easy-to-navigate grid system with narrow two- and three-storey houses, in which each room has a window looking over the street, it has housed fishermen and workers since the 18th century.

In the small Plaça de la Barceloneta is the Baroque church of Sant Miquel del Port, which was also designed

↑ Strolling along the wooden boardwalk at Port Vell marina

by Cermeño. The square itself is dominated by a popular covered market.

Today, Barceloneta's fishing fleet is still based in the nearby Moll del Rellotge (the clock dock), where stands a small clock tower. On the opposite side of this harbour is the Torre de Sant Sebastià, terminus of the cable car that runs right across the port, via the World Trade Centre, to the garden-filled slopes of Montjuïc.

Aquàrium

G9 **Moll d'Espanya** **Barceloneta, Drassanes** **Hours vary, check website** **aquariumbcn.com**

Populated by over 11,000 creatures belonging to 450 different species, Barcelona's aquarium is one of the biggest in Europe. The three-storey glass aquarium focuses particularly on the marine life of the local Mediterranean coast. Two of Catalonia's nature reserves, the southern Delta de L'Ebre (p198) and the

Medes isles off the Costa Brava, are given a tank apiece. Tropical seas are also represented and moving platforms ferry visitors through a glass tunnel under an "ocean" filled with toothy sharks, soaring rays and bright schools of sunfish. A large hall provides ample space for children's activities, including an island reached via crawl-through glass tunnels.

STAY

The Serras Hotel Barcelona
Youthful Serras is a firm favourite of those in the know. Perks include a rooftop plunge pool.

G8 **Passeig de Colom 9** **hotelthe serrasbarcelona.com**

€€€

Chic & Basic Born
Great style on a budget, this 19th-century townhouse has small, cleverly designed rooms.

H7 **Calle Princessa 50** **chicandbasic.com**

€€€

Banys Orientals
Pick one of the compact but inviting rooms, with modern four-poster beds and romantic lighting.

H7 **Calle Argenteria 37** **hotelbanys orientals.com**

€€€

↑ Sharks and schools of fish swim above the glass tunnels of the Aquàrium

A sandy beach stretching along the city's coast

↑ A complete replica of the *Real,* housed in the *(inset)* Museu Marítim and Drassanes

Museu Marítim and Drassanes

📍 F8 🏛 Avinguda de les Drassanes Ⓜ Drassanes 🕐 10am–8pm daily ✖ 1 & 6 Jan, 25 & 26 Dec 🌐 mmb.cat

The great galleys that were instrumental in making Barcelona a major seafaring power were built in the sheds of the Drassanes (shipyards). Today, the shipyards house the maritime museum, a sprawling exhibition space covering more than 10,000 sq m

(108,000 sq ft) and fronted by glass windows. The docks were founded in the mid-13th century, when dynastic marriages uniting the kingdoms of Sicily and Aragón meant that better maritime communications between the two became a priority. Three of the yards' four original corner towers survive. Indeed these royal dry docks are now the largest and most complete surviving medieval complex of their kind in the world.

Among the vessels to slip from the Drassanes' vaulted halls was the *Real,* flagship of Don Juan of Austria, who led the Christian fleet to the famous victory against the Turks at Lepanto in 1571. The

undoubted highlight of the museum's collection is a full-scale replica of the *Real* decorated in red and gold. The renovated halls also host temporary exhibitions with a maritime theme, as well as displaying other historic boats created right in these ship-yards. With many 18th- to 20th-century instruments preserved in their permanent collection, visitors can also track the development of nautical navigation tools from the sextant to the depth gauge.

Included in the admission fee is an audio guide of the museum's collections, as well as a visit to the *Santa Eulàlia* (p91), a restored century-old schooner moored in Port Vell.

> **Among the vessels to slip from the Drassanes' vaulted halls was the *Real,* flagship of Don Juan of Austria, who led the Christian fleet to the famous victory against the Turks at Lepanto in 1517.**

28

Mirador de Colom

📍 F8 🏛 Plaça del Portal de la Pau 📞 932 85 38 54 Ⓜ Drassanes 🕐 Mar–Sep: 8:30am–8:30pm daily, Oct–Feb: 8:30am–7:30pm daily

The Columbus monument at the bottom of La Rambla (p72) was designed by Gaietà Buigas for the 1888 Universal

Exhibition, when Catalans considered the explorer a Catalan rather than an Italian. The bronze statue of the explorer atop the column was designed by Rafael Atché.

The towering monument marks the spot where Columbus stepped ashore in 1493 after returning from his voyage to the Caribbean. He brought with him six indigenous Caribbeans and he was given a state welcome by the Catholic monarchs in the vast, arched Saló del Tinell of the Plaça del Rei (p80). The subsequent conversion of the Caribbeans to Christianity is commemorated by a plaque in Barcelona's cathedral (p70).

A lift leads to a viewing platform at the top of the monument, from where visitors can take in panoramic vistas across the city. Back on the ground, visitors can also enjoy wine tasting in the monument's cellar. A combined ticket for both the lift and the tasting can be purchased at the base of the monument.

Mirador de Colom, a 19th-century statue of the famous explorer

↑ The pleasant, honey-coloured exterior of the Museu d'Història de Catalunya

29 ♻ 🐾

Museu d'Història de Catalunya

📍H8 🏠Plaça Pau Vila 3 🚇Barceloneta, Drassanes 🕐10am-7pm Tue & Thu-Sat, 10am-8pm Wed, 10am-2:30pm Sun & public hols 🚫1 & 6 Jan, 1 May, 10 Jun, 25 & 26 Dec 🌐mhcat.cat

Charting the long history of Catalonia, this fascinating museum explores the region from Lower Palaeolithic times to its heyday as a maritime power and industrial pioneer. On the second floor, exhibits include the Moorish invasion, Romanesque architecture (p176), medieval monastic life and the rise of Catalan seafaring. Third-floor exhibits cover the industrial revolution and the impact of steam power and electricity on the economy. Here visitors can step into the shoes of yesterday's Catalans by trying on medieval armour or climbing aboard a 1920s tram that once ran through the city. The first floor is reserved for temporary exhibits. A free guide supplies exhibit information in English.

On the fourth floor is the café-restaurant. Note that you do not need to have a ticket to the museum to sample the menu of tasty seafood dishes, which are served alongside beautiful views over the yacht-filled port from the huge terrace.

CHRISTOPHER COLUMBUS

The renowned explorer was born in Genoa in 1451. Sponsored by Spain's King Ferdinand and Queen Isabella on his first voyage across the Atlantic in 1492, he became the first European to discover the New World. Columbus died in Valladolid in 1506, and his tomb is today in Seville's cathedral.

A SHORT WALK
BARRI GÒTIC

Distance 1 km (0.5 miles) **Nearest metro**
Jaume I **Time** 15 minutes

The Barri Gòtic (Gothic Quarter) is the true heart of
Barcelona. The oldest part of the city, it was the site chosen
by the Romans in the reign of Augustus (27 BC–AD 14) on
which to found a new *colonia* (town), and has been the
location of the city's administrative buildings ever
since. The Roman forum was on the Plaça de Sant
Jaume, where the medieval Palau de la
Generalitat, Catalonia's parliament, and the
Ajuntament, Barcelona's town hall, now
stand. A walk around the area also takes in
the Gothic cathedral and royal palace,
where Columbus was received by
Fernando and Isabel on his return from
his voyage to the New World in 1492.

Built on the Roman city wall, **Casa
de l'Ardiaca***, the Gothic-
Renaissance arch-deacon's
residence, now houses the city's
historical archives (p81).*

*The façade and spire are 20th-century
additions to the original Gothic*
Cathedral *(p70). Among the treasures
inside are medieval Catalan paintings.*

The seat of Catalonia's governor, the **Palau
de la Generalitat** *(p82) has superb Gothic
features, including a stone staircase rising
to an open-air, arcaded gallery.*

To La Rambla

SANT SEVER

SANT DOMÈNEC DEL CALL

SANT HONORAT

CARRER DEL BISBE

PIE

PLAÇA DE
SANT JAUME

C. DE FERRAN

The **Ajuntament,**
*Barcelona's town hall,
may have a Neo-
Classical façade, but
this was only a later
addition to the original
14th-century
building (p70).*

CARRER DE LA CIUTAT

↑ The intricate 20th-century
façade and spire of
Barcelona Cathedral

0 metres   100
0 yards   100   N ↗

Locator Map
For more detail see p68

↑ Walking under the arches in the internal courtyard of the Museu Frederic Marès

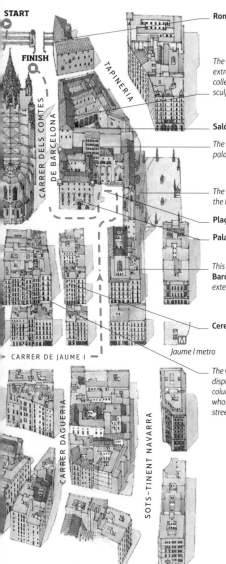

START

FINISH

Roman city wall

The mainstay of the **Museu Frederic Marès** extraordinarily eclectic and high-quality collections is the extensive display of Spanish sculpture (p81).

Saló del Tinell

The **MUHBA Plaça del Rei**, the former royal palace, has a dramatic exterior (p80).

The **Capella Reial de Santa Àgata** is one of the highlights of the MUHBA Plaça del Rei.

Plaça del Rei

Palau del Lloctinent

This section of **MUHBA (Museu d'Història de Barcelona)** features the world's most extensive subterranean Roman ruins.

Cereria Subirà *candle shop*

Jaume I metro

The **Centre Excursionista de Catalunya** displays in its entrance courtyard Roman columns from the Temple of Augustus, whose site is marked by a millstone in the street outside.

Did You Know?

The Temple of Augustus was discovered during building work in the 19th century.

A LONG WALK
EL BORN

Distance 1.5 km (1 mile) **Nearest metro**
Jaume I **Time** 30 minutes

The tiny district of El Born, across the Via Laietana from
the Barrí Gotic, has made a comeback. Close to the
waterfront, it flourished in Catalonia's mercantile heyday
from the 13th century. The narrow streets still bear the
names of the craftsmen and guilds that set up here. While
it retains some medieval air, El Born is a lively place to be.

Locator Map
For more detail see p68

OLD
TOWN   El Born

PLAÇA DE
L'ANGEL

*From Jaume I metro station
in Plaça de l'Angel,
set off on a walk down
Carrer de l'Argenteria.*

M Jaume I
START

CARRER DE LA BORIA

CARRER DE LA PRINCESA

C. DELS
COTONERS

C. D
BARRA
FERR

CARRER DEL VIGATANS

FINISH

*There is a carved head
protruding from the wall on
the right at the corner of
Carrer dels Mirallers.*

Bodega Loca *is one of a handful of
old-fashioned taverns that have remained
unchanged for decades.*

*The charming **Plaça de
Santa Maria** is a perfect
place for a coffee or a glass
of wine on a café terrace.*

VIA

LAIETANA

CARRER DE L'ARGENTERIA

CARRER DE GRUNYÍ

CARRER DE BANYS VELLS

CARRER DELS MIRALLERS

CARRER DE

CARRER DE LA NAU

PLAÇA DE
VÍCTOR
BALAGUER

Bode
Loc

C. DELS

PLAÇA DE
SANTA MARIA

C. L'ESPA

CARRER DELS
CANVIS VELLS

La
Llotja

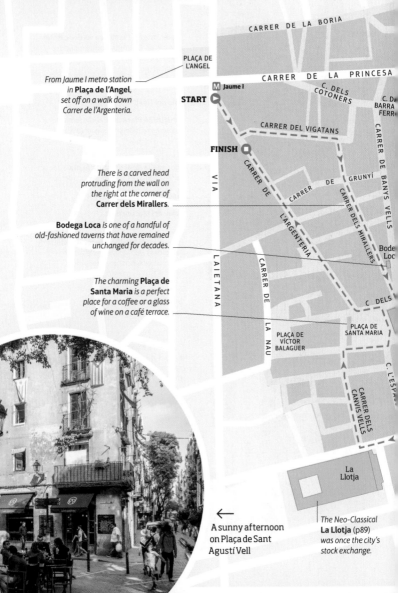

← A sunny afternoon
on Plaça de Sant
Agustí Vell

*The Neo-Classical
La Llotja (p89)
was once the city's
stock exchange.*

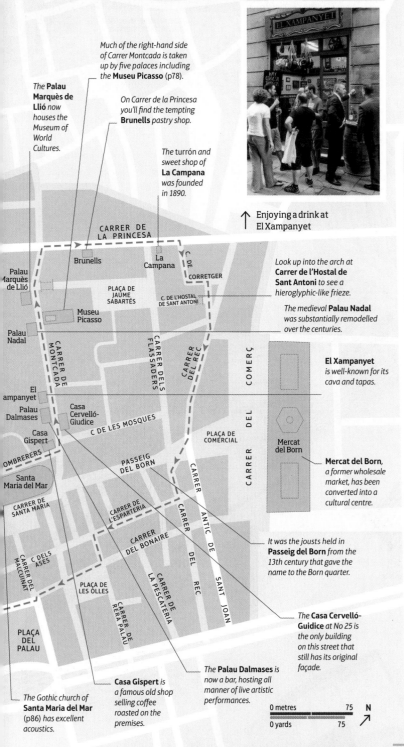

Much of the right-hand side of Carrer Montcada is taken up by five palaces including the **Museu Picasso** (p78).

The **Palau Marquès de Lió** now houses the Museum of World Cultures.

On Carrer de la Princesa you'll find the tempting **Brunells** pastry shop.

The turrón and sweet shop of **La Campana** was founded in 1890.

Enjoying a drink at El Xampanyet

CARRER DE LA PRINCESA

Brunells

La Campana

C. DE CORRETGER

Palau Marquès de Lió

PLAÇA DE JAUME SABARTÉS

C. DE L'HOSTAL DE SANT ANTONI

Museu Picasso

Palau Nadal

Look up into the arch at **Carrer de l'Hostal de Sant Antoni** to see a hieroglyphic-like frieze.

The medieval **Palau Nadal** was substantially remodelled over the centuries.

CARRER DE MONTCADA

CARRER DELS FLASSADERS

CARRER DEL REC

CARRER DEL COMERÇ

El Xampanyet

El Xampanyet is well-known for its cava and tapas.

Palau Dalmases

Casa Cervelló-Giudice

C DE LES MOSQUES

PLAÇA DE COMERCIAL

CARRER DEL

Mercat del Born

Casa Gispert

OMBRERERS

Santa Maria del Mar

Mercat del Born, a former wholesale market, has been converted into a cultural centre.

PASSEIG DEL BORN

CARRER DE SANTA MARIA

CARRER DE L'ESPARTERIA

CARRER DEL BONAIRE

CARRER ANTIC DE SANT JOAN

It was the jousts held in **Passeig del Born** from the 13th century that gave the name to the Born quarter.

C DELS ASES

CARRER DEL MALCUINAT

PLAÇA DE LES OLLES

CARRER DE LA PESCATERIA

CARRER DEL REC

The **Casa Cervelló-Giudice** at No 25 is the only building on this street that still has its original façade.

PLAÇA DEL PALAU

CARRER DE RERA PALAU

The Gothic church of **Santa Maria del Mar** (p86) has excellent acoustics.

Casa Gispert is a famous old shop selling coffee roasted on the premises.

The **Palau Dalmases** is now a bar, hosting all manner of live artistic performances.

0 metres 75
0 yards 75
N

EIXAMPLE

Barcelona claims to have the greatest collection of Art Nouveau buildings of any city in Europe. The style, known in Catalonia as Modernisme, flourished after 1854, when the government decided to pull down the medieval walls to allow the city to develop into what had previously been a military zone. The designs of the civil engineer Ildefons Cerdà i Sunyer were chosen for the new expansion *(eixample)* inland. These plans called for a rigid grid system of streets, but at each intersection, the corners were chamfered, with their corners cut off at a 45° angle, to allow the buildings there to overlook the junctions or squares. The Modernistes, however, had other ideas for this new land, as seen in the Diagonal, a main avenue that runs from the wealthy area of Pedralbes down to the sea, and the Hospital de la Santa Creu i Sant Pau by architect Domènech i Montaner. He hated the grid system and deliberately angled the hospital to look down the diagonal Avinguda de Gaudí towards Antoni Gaudí's church of the Sagrada Família. The wealth of Barcelona's commercial elite and their passion for all things new allowed them to give free rein to the age's most innovative architects in designing their residences, as well as public buildings, creating a unique cityscape.

In the late 20th century, a multitude of shops, bars, clubs and restaurants catering to the LGBT+ community sprang up in this fashionable area, earning it the nickname "Gaixample".

EIXAMPLE

Must Sees
1 Sagrada Família
2 Casa Batlló
3 La Pedrera

Experience More
4 Illa de la Discòrdia
5 Fundació Antoni Tàpies
6 Recinte Modernista de Sant Pau
7 Fundació Mapfre
8 Casa Terrades
9 Museu del Modernisme Català
10 Museu de la Música
11 Museu Egipci de Barcelona

Eat
① El Nacional
② Mordisco
③ Casa Calvet
④ Moments

Drink
⑤ Dry Martini
⑥ Chill Bar
⑦ Milano

Stay
⑧ Hotel Constanza
⑨ Cotton House Hotel

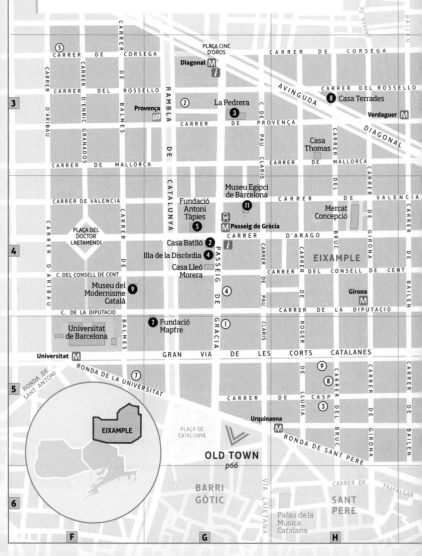

1 ⚜ Ⓜ

SAGRADA FAMÍLIA

Ⓠ K3 **Ⓐ** Carrer de Sardenya **Ⓜ** Sagrada Família **🚌** 19, 43, 51 **Ⓞ** Apr–Sep: 9am–8pm daily; Oct & Mar: 9am–7pm daily; Nov–Feb: 9am–6pm daily (to 2pm 1 & 6 Jan, 25 & 26 Dec); timed tickets only, advance booking advisable **Ⓦ** sagradafamilia.org

Europe's most unconventional church, the Temple Expiatori de la Sagrada Família is an emblem of the city. Crammed with symbolism inspired by nature and striving for originality, it is Gaudí's greatest work and one of the finest examples of Modernisme.

Architect Francesc de Paula Villar i Lozano was initially charged with building a Christian temple in Barcelona. Envisioning a Gothic-style building, he drew up plans for a three-nave church. In 1883, a year after work had begun on a Neo-Gothic church on the site, the task of completing it was given to the 31-year-old Gaudí, who changed everything, extemporizing as he went along. He designed it, like a medieval cathedral, to be considered like a book in stone, with each element representing a Biblical event or aspect of Christian faith. It became his life's work and he lived like a recluse on the site for 14 years. At his death (he is buried in the crypt) only one tower on the Nativity façade had been completed, but work resumed after the Civil War and several more have since been finished according to his original plans. Work continues today, financed by public subscription.

> **Crammed with symbolism inspired by nature and striving for originality, it is Gaudí's greatest work and one of the finest examples of Modernisme.**

↑ People attending a Mass in the Sagrada Família's soaring nave

Timeline

1866
△ Josep Maria Bocabella founded the Association of Saint Joseph Devout, with the aim to build a temple in the city.

1887
△ The vicarage is completed. This building becomes Gaudí's work space and is where he spent his last years.

1954
△ Work begins on the Passion façade, 62 years after it began on the Nativity façade.

2017
△ On the 135th anniversary of the laying of the foundation stone, 70 per cent of the basilica was finished.

PICTURE PERFECT
Mirror, Mirror on the Floor

The Plaça de Gaudí offers one of the best views of the Sagrada Família. From this garden, you can capture a great shot of the basilica reflected in the lake.

↑ The unique exterior of the Sagrada Família reflected in Plaça de Gaudí's lake

Exploring the Sagrada Família

Gaudí's masterpiece seemingly climbs closer to the heavens as the years progress, its mosaic-covered towers reaching towards the clouds. Of the three decorated façades, the Nativity (p110) and Passion (p111) have been completed, while the Glory is still a work in progress.

The interior of the basilica more than matches the mesmerizing exterior. Soaring pilars form a canopy-like roof and jewel-hued stained-glass creates pools of light on the floor of the nave, giving the effect of walking across a magical forest's floor. The experience culminates at the main altar, which is drenched in natural light. It's a profound expression of the architect's devotion, and a challenge to even the firmest of non-believers to remain unmoved.

After touring the nave and climbing one of the towers, explore the museum in the crypt. Charting Gaudí's career and the development of the basilica, it ends at the foot of his tomb.

2026

The date that the basilica is set to be completed.

Spiral staircases

Towers with lift

Eight of the 12 decorated bell towers, one for each apostle, have been built.

The altar canopy was designed by Gaudí.

The apse was the first part of the church Gaudí completed. Stairs lead down from here to the crypt below.

The crypt, where Gaudí is buried, was begun by the original architect, Francisco de Paula del Villar i Lozano, in 1882.

GREAT VIEW
Get Low

Lie down on the floor of the nave and look up at the ceiling for a unique view of Gaudí's fantastical creation. Does it look like a vibrant coral reef or the inside of a colourful kaleidoscope?

The controversial Passion façade was crafted from 1986 to 2000. Its sculpted figures are angular and often sinister.

① Stained-glass windows bathe the nave in multi-coloured pools of light.

② Spiral staircases lead you to the top of the bell towers, where you'll be rewarded with amazing views of the city.

③ The nave's roof is held up by soaring pilars that branch out at the top to form a canopy.

Finished in 1930, the Nativity façade has doorways which represent Faith, Hope and Charity. Scenes of the Nativity and Christ's childhood are embellished with symbolism.

The nave contains a forest of fluted pillars that support four galleries above the side aisles; a large number of skylights let in both natural and artificial light.

←
Illustration depicting the magnificent Sagrada Família in 2020

THE FINISHED CHURCH

Gaudí's initial ambitions have been fulfilled over the years, using various new technologies to achieve his vision. Still to come is the central tower, which is to be encircled by four large towers representing the Evangelists. Four towers on the Glory (south) façade will match the existing four on the Passion (west) and Nativity (east) façades. An ambulatory - like an inside-out cloister - will skirt the outside of the building.

↑ The soaring bell towers on the honeycomb-like Nativity façade

NATIVITY FAÇADE

Finished according to Gaudí's instructions before his death, the lavish ornamentation on the eastern façade centres around three doors dedicated to Hope (left), Faith (right) and Charity, in the middle.

Hope Doorway

Above this door you'll see Joseph and the child Jesus watched over by Mary's parents, St Ann and St Joachim. The lintel of the door is composed of a woodcutter's two-handled saw and various other tools – all indicative of Joseph's profession.

The spire above the doorway is in the form of an elongated boulder, which is an allusion to the holy Catalan mountain of Montserrat (p154). At the base of this

Did You Know?

The chameleons on this façade represent change, while the turtle signifies stability.

boulder sits Joseph in a boat; he bears a resemblance to Gaudí himself and is very likely a posthumous homage.

Faith Doorway

The heart of Jesus can be seen set into the lintel above this doorway. The scene on the lower left is the Visitation by Mary to Elizabeth, her cousin and mother of John the Baptist. On the right, Jesus wields a hammer and chisel in his father's workshop.

As it rises, the stonework forms an intricate pinnacle recording the fundamentals of Catholicism, including a lamp with three wicks for the Trinity, bunches of grapes and ears of wheat for the Eucharist, and a hand set with an eye, showing God's omniscience.

Charity Doorway

These double doors are separated by a column

recording Jesus's genealogy. The three Magi are on the lower left of the door, with the shepherds opposite them. Out of the Nativity emerges the spiky tail of a many-pointed star, surrounded by a children's choir. Above the star is the Annunciation and the Coronation of the Virgin Mary by Jesus, and on top of that is a pelican sitting on a crown next to a glass egg bearing the JHS monogram of Jesus.

GLORY FAÇADE

The southern façade is set to be the most monumental of the four and, based on Gaudí's plans, will represent the road to God. A large staircase decorated with demons and tombs will lead to the façade, signifying death. The seven pillars supporting the structure will depict the seven sins at the bottom, and the seven virtues at the top, and the seven doors signify the sacraments that open the way to God. Clouds will rise up the bell towers to a glorious image of God.

↑ Stone depiction of the shepherds above the Charity doorway

PASSION FAÇADE

The Passion façade narrates Christ's final days leading up to the Crucifixion. Designed by Josep Maria Subirachs, whose boxy forms are very unlike the organic shapes on the Gaudí-designed Nativity façade, the Passion façade has divided critics since its completion.

Christ's Passion

The Passion façade depicts the sufferings and execution of Jesus, and its style reflects its subject matter. The statuary has attracted criticism for its angular, "dehumanized" carving, but Gaudí would probably have approved. He is known to have favoured an Expressionist style to give the story of Christ's Passion maximum impact. A great porch, whose roof is held up by six inclined, buttress-like swamp tree roots, shades the 12 groups of sculptures. The first scene (bottom left-hand corner) is the Last Supper at which Jesus (standing) announces his impending betrayal. Next to this is the arrest in the Garden of Gethsemane. The kiss of betrayal by Judas follows. The numbers of the cryptogram to the side of Jesus add up to 33 in every direction: his age at the time of his death.

↑ Bronze door carved with the gospel on the Passion façade

The Flagellation

In the Flagellation (between the central doors) Jesus is shown tied to a column at the top of a flight of three steps representing the three days of the Passion. Peter denying Christ is indicated by the cock that will crow three times in fulfilment of Jesus' prophecy. Behind is a labyrinth, a metaphor for Jesus' fate.

The sculptural group on the bottom right shows Christ bound and crowned with thorns. Pilate, overlooked by the Roman eagle, is seen washing his hands, freeing himself of responsibility for Jesus' death. Above, the Three Marys weep as Simon of Cyrene is told by the Romans to pick up the cross.

HIDDEN GEM
School Spirit
To the right of the Passion façade you'll find the Escoles de Gaudí, which the architect designed to be a school. Today, the undulating brick roof shelters a re-creation of Gaudí's office, with displays exploring his craft and aesthetic.

The Holy Shroud

The central sculpture depicts an event not described in the Bible. Veronica holds up her head cloth, which she has offered to Jesus to wipe the blood and sweat from his face. It has been returned, impressed with his likeness.

Next comes a Roman centurion on horseback piercing the side of Jesus with his sword. Above him, three soldiers beneath the cross cast lots for Jesus' tunic. The largest sculpture (top centre) shows Christ hanging from a horizontal cross. At his feet is a skull referring to the place of the Crucifixion, Golgotha. Above him is the veil of the Temple of Jerusalem. The final scene is the burial of Jesus. The figure of Nicodemus, who is anointing the body, is thought to be a self-portrait.

→ Haunting sculptural figures on the Passion façade depicting Peter's betrayal of Jesus

CASA BATLLÓ

📍 G4 🏛 Passeig de Gràcia 43 🕐 9am-9pm daily
🚇 Passeig de Gràcia 🌐 casabatllo.es

With its reworked façade of stunning organic forms – both inside and out – and its fantastic chimneys and rooftop, Casa Batlló remains as bold and convention-defying today as it did when it was finished in 1906.

Unlike Gaudí's other works, this block of flats on the prestigious Passeig de Gràcia involved the conversion of an existing structure. The building, commissioned by Josep Batlló i Casanovas, has been said to symbolise the legend of St George killing the dragon, whose scaly back arches above the main façade. The spindly columns across the first-floor windows have since been compared to tibias (lower leg bones), earning Casa Batlló the nickname "House of Bones". Inside, highlights include the blue-hued light-well, the skeleton-like attics and the mushroom-shaped fireplace. It was designated a UNESCO World Heritage Site in 2005.

Did You Know?

Salvador Dalí said that the curving walls and windows represent "waves on a stormy day".

Tightly packed and abstractly patterned chimneys, which have become Gaudí's trademark

Attics

Patio and rear façade, with its cast-iron balconies and superbly colourful trencadís work at the top

The dining room ceiling is rippled with bulbous forms that are thought to represent the splash caused by a drop of water.

Stairs to main floor

← The exterior of Casa Batlló, tiled in green and blue

The light-well provides maximum light to interior windows.

1 The closely packed brick arches of the attics are plastered and painted white, giving the sensation of being inside the skeleton of a large animal.

2 One side of the main drawing room is formed of stained-glass windows looking out over the Passeig de Gràcia.

3 The house is topped with close-packed, spectacularly patterned chimneys.

The Dragon's Back, an incredible narrow, colourfully tiled cap above the façade

Dragon's Belly room

A damaged ceramic cross, which Gaudí refused to send for repair as he liked the cracked effect

The mask-like iron balconies

Trencadís decorations

← A look inside Gaudí's intriguing 20th-century Casa Batlló

Main drawing room

Fireplace room was Josep Batlló's office and has a mushroom-shaped fireplace.

People walking among the sculptural chimneys on La Pedrera's undulating roof ↑

3 ✍️

LA PEDRERA

📍G3 🚇Passeig de Gràcia 92 🚇Diagonal 🕐Mar-Oct & 26 Dec-3 Jan: 9am-8:30pm daily; Nov-Feb: 9am-6:30pm daily, except 26 Dec-3 Jan; Pedrera Origins: Mar-Oct & 26 Dec-3 Jan: 9-11pm daily; Nov-Feb: 7-9pm daily 🚫25 Dec 🌐lapedrera.com

There isn't a single straight line in La Pedrera, Gaudí's extraordinary apartment building – the façade ripples like water. The rooftop terrace, with its tiled chimneys and undulating walkways, is one of the city's most popular attractions.

Sometimes called Casa Milà, La Pedrera was Gaudí's last work before he devoted himself entirely to the Sagrada Família (p106). Built between 1906 and 1912 for Pere Milà, a wealthy industrialist, La Pedrera completely departed from the construction principles of the time and, as a result, it was strongly attacked by Barcelona's intellectuals. On its completion, it was greeted with both horror and amusement, and was quickly nicknamed "'La Pedrera", meaning "the quarry", for its wavy façade of undressed stone.

Here you'll visit a restored apartment, as well as the two circular courtyards, before exploring the Gaudí Exhibition on the top floor. The culmination of the visit is the stunning roof terrace, where jazz concerts are held in the summer among the peculiar air ducts and chimneys.

> 💬 INSIDER TIP
> **Light Bulb Moment**
>
> Book a night tour to see La Pedrera come to life during Pedrera Origins, a spectacular sound and light show held on the roof. After watching the show, you'll enjoy a glass of cava and a plate of sweetmeats.

[1] The intricate iron-work balconies by Josep Maria Jujol look like seaweed against La Pedrera's wave-like walls of white undressed stone.

[2] In the "Whale Attic", the Gaudí Exhibition displays the architect's drawings and models to explain the aesthetics of his designs.

[3] The many sculpted air ducts and chimneys on the roof have been dubbed both the "garden of warriors" and "*espanta-bruixes*" ("witch-scarers").

GAIXAMPLE EXPERIENCES

Night Barcelona
A buzzing bar that regularly hosts photography exhibitions.
🆆 nightbarcelona.net

Axel Hotel
The world's first hotel chain aimed specifically at LGBT+ travellers.
🆆 axelhotels.com

dDivine
Mediterranean food meets drag shows at this pink-lit restaurant.
🆆 ddivine.com

Rainbow Gay Tours
Take an expert-led private tour of the area's nightlife and restaurants.
🆆 rainbowgaytours.com

EXPERIENCE MORE

4 (Ⓜ)

Illa de la Discòrdia

📍 G4 🏠 Passeig de Gràcia, between Carrer d'Aragó and Carrer del Consell de Cent 🚇 Passeig de Gràcia

Barcelona's most famous group of Modernista *(p36)* buildings illustrates the wide range of styles used by the movement's architects. They lie in an area known as the Illa de la Discòrdia (Block of Discord), in a nod to the startling visual clash between them. The three finest were remodelled in the early 1900s in the Modernista style from existing houses.

At No.35 Passeig de Gràcia, a shop was installed in the ground floor of **Casa Lleó Morera** (1902–6), Lluís Domènech i Montaner's first residential work, in 1943, but upstairs the exquisite Modernista interiors have been perfectly preserved. The house is currently closed to the public, but you can still admire the façade and the magnificent stained-glass windows from the outside.

Three doors down is **Casa Amatller**, designed by Josep Puig i Cadafalch in 1898. Its façade, under a stepped-gable roof, features a harmonious blend of Moorish and Gothic windows. The entrance patio, with its spiral columns and staircase covered by a stained-glass skylight, can be seen at any time; the rest of the building, including the lovely wood-panelled library, can only be seen on a guided tour. On the ground floor you'll find a lively café specializing in chocolate baked treats, located in the former kitchen, and the shop of a renowned jewellers.

Also in the block is Antoni Gaudí's Casa Batlló *(p112)*, with its fluid façade evoking marine or natural forms. The bizarrely decorated chimney became a trademark of Gaudí's later work.

Casa Lleó Morera
☺ 🏠 Passeig de Gràcia 35 🚇 To the public 🆆 casalleomorera.com

Casa Amatller
Ⓐ Ⓜ ☺ 🖻 🏠 Passeig de Gràcia 41 🕙 10am–6pm daily 🆆 amatller.org

Did You Know?

Passeig de Gràcia is the considered home of the most expensive real estate in Barcelona.

↑ The stunning stained-glass windows of Casa Lleó Morera

Fundació Antoni Tàpies

🔲 G4 🏠 Carrer d'Aragó 255 🚇 Passeig de Gràcia 🕐 10am-7pm Tue-Thu & Sat, 10am-9pm Fri, 10am-3pm Sun 🚫 1 & 6 Jan, 25 Dec 🌐 fundaciotapies.org

Before he died in 2012, Antoni Tàpies was one of Barcelona's best-known contemporary artists. Strongly inspired by Surrealism, he used a variety of materials in his abstract work, including concrete and metal. The exhibits at the *fundació* provide a comprehensive overview of his work. The collection is housed in Barcelona's first domestic building to be constructed using iron, designed by Barcelona-born Domènech i Montaner in 1880 for his brother's publishing firm.

EAT

El Nacional
This gastro temple hosts a plethora of bars and restaurants offering everything from fresh oysters to regional charcuterie.

🔲 G5 🏠 Passeig de Gràcia 24 Bis 🌐 elnacionalbcn.com

€€€

Mordisco
Head here for modern interpretations of classic Catalan cuisine, dished up within a light-drenched atrium.

🔲 G3 🏠 Passatge de la Concepció 10 🌐 grupotragaluz.com

€€€

Casa Calvet
Catalan food with a modern twist is served in these dining rooms, beautifully designed by Antoni Gaudí.

🔲 H5 🏠 Carrer de Casp 48 ☎ 93 412 40 12

€€€

Moments
The interiors of this hotel restaurant are as slick as the Michelin-starred food. Try the tasting menu for a truly luxurious experience.

🔲 G4 🏠 Passeig de Gràcia 38-40 🚫 Sun & Mon 🌐 mandarin oriental.com

€€€

↑ Fundació Antoni Tàpies, topped with a cloud of wire

DRINK

Dry Martini

A bewitchingly old-school cocktail bar, with formal service and an uber modern menu.

Q F3 **A** Carrer d'Aribau 162 **W** drymartini org.com

Chill Bar

Choose from a well-curated wine list at this laid-back refuge near Sagrada Família.

Q K3 **A** Carrer de Provença 424 **W** chillbarcelona.com

Milano

Enjoy expertly made cocktails and live jazz at this oasis of elegance and calm.

Q F5 **A** Ronda de la Universitat 35 **W** camparimilano.com

---

6 ⊘ ⊗

Recinte Modernista de Sant Pau

Q L2 **A** Carrer de Sant Antoni Maria Claret 167 **⊕** Sant Pau - Dos de Maig **⊙** Apr-Oct: 9:30am-7pm Mon-Sat, 9:30am-3pm Sun; Nov-Mar: 9:30am-5pm Mon-Sat, 9:30am-3pm Sun **W** santpaubarcelona.org

Lluís Domènech i Montaner began designing this former city hospital in 1902. His innovative scheme consisted of 26 attractive Mudéjar-style pavilions set in large gardens, as he believed that patients would recover better among fresh air and trees. Also believing art and colour to be therapeutic, he decorated the pavilions profusely; the reception pavilion has mosaic murals and sculptures by Pau Gargallo. All the connecting corridors and service areas were hidden underground. After Domènech i Montaner's death, the project was completed in 1930 by his son, Pere. The buildings are now used for cultural activities.

---

7 ⊘ ⊗

Fundación Mapfre

Q G5 **A** Carrer de la Diputació 250 **⊕** Passeig de Gràcia **⊙** 2-8pm Mon, 10am-8pm Tue-Sat, 11am-7pm Sun **W** fundacion mapfre.org

The Fundación Mapfre's exhibition space is housed in the Casa Garriga Nogués, a beautiful mansion designed by Enric Sagnier in a blend of Rococo, Neo-Classical and Modernista styles. The house was completed in 1902 for the wealthy Garriga Nogués banking family, who gave the building its name. Its wide balcony along the façade is supported by four striking columns, designed by sculptor Eusebi Arnau, representing the four stages of life.

Inside, light pours into the sumptuous galleries from a stunning stained-glass ceiling, creating an elegant setting for a rolling programme of well-curated temporary exhibitions

Every Friday in June, the Recinte Modernista Sant Pau hosts concerts in its gardens. You can listen to a range of different musicians in the atmospheric dusk light, surrounded by the glowing buildings.

of mid-19th- to mid-20th-century painting, and modern photography. Although there have been a few blockbuster exhibitions – most notably one on Impressionism in 2018 that featured works loaned from the Musée d'Orsay in Paris – most concentrate on lesser known, typically Catalan artists and photographers.

The museum also promotes community building, from cookery classes for children to grants for projects helping people in need. Guided tours of the museum are given in Catalan and Spanish. Audio guides in other languages are also available, albeit for a small fee. Entry is free on Mondays.

↑ Exploring an exhibit housed within a curved tower of the Casa Terrades

Casa Terrades

◻ H3 **◻ Avinguda Diagonal 420** **◻ Diagonal** **◻ 10am–7pm daily** **◻ casadeles punxes.com**

This free-standing, six-sided apartment block by Catalan Modernista architect Josep Puig i Cadafalch gets its nickname, Casa de les Punxes (House of the Points), from the spires on its six corner turrets. A conversion of three existing houses, completed between 1903 and 1905, the building is an eclectic mixture of medieval and Renaissance styles. The towers and gables are influenced in particular by the Gothic architecture of northern Europe. However, the floral stone ornamentation of the exterior, in combination with the predominant use of red brick, are typically Modernista.

↑ The splendid buildings of the Recinte Modernista de Sant Pau, bright with mosaics

↑ Furniture and *(inset)* stained glass on display at the Museu del Modernisme Català

Museu del Modernisme Català

♀F4 ⬆ Calle de Balmes 48 ⬆ Passeig de Gràcia ⏰ 10:30am–2pm & 4–7pm Mon–Fri 🚫 Aug 🌐 mmbcn.cat

This museum claims to be the only one in Europe dedicated entirely to Catalan Art Nouveau. Suitably situated in a Modernista mansion, designed by Enric Sagnier, this private collection features an impressive array of paintings, furnishings, sculptures and decorative arts gathered by local antique dealers over the last half century.

The top floor displays the furniture collection. Here an entire gallery is dedicated to pieces by Gaudí, including a delightful kissing chair. Sculptures by Josep Llimona

are also afforded their own space, as are paintings by Ramon Casas – one of the founders of the Els 4 Gats tavern *(p37)*, which hosted Picasso's first exhibition – as well as a series of original Modernista posters.

Beyond this permanent collection, the museum hosts temporary exhibits as well as workshops, concerts, and family activities. There's a small café where visitors can enjoy coffee or pastries while sitting amid typical Modernista decoration.

Museu de la Música

♀L5 ⬆ L'Auditori, Calle Lepant 150 ⬆ Marina, Glòries ⏰ 10am–6pm Tue, Wed & Fri, 10am–9pm Thu, 10am–7pm Sat & Sun 🌐 ajuntament.barcelona. cat/museumusica/ca

Barcelona's fascinating music museum is located in L'Auditori concert hall. As well as regular temporary exhibits, the permanent collection contains more than 2,200

instruments from all over the world. At any one time, around 500 of these are on display in red velvet cases. Ranging from 17th-century lutes to Indian sitars to Japanese kotos, the exhibits are complemented by audiovisuals, interactive screens and listening stations that explain the history of music from the Middle Ages right up to the present day, and the evolution of musical cultures from around the world. The museum also

TOP 3 CATALAN MUSICIANS

Montserrat Caballé
A soprano best known for her soaring duet with Freddie Mercury, *Barcelona*, which was played at the 1992 Olympics.

Pau Casals
Known in English as Pablo Casals, he was one of the greatest cellists of the 20th century.

José Carreras
Born in Barcelona in 1946, Carreras is one of the famous "Three Tenors", alongside Plácido Domingo and Luciano Pavarotti.

explores how music has been recorded over time, displaying various forms of notation on manuscript paper next to contemporary audio recording equipment.

The undisputed highlight of the music museum, however, is the world-class collection of classical guitars, including pieces made by Antonio de Torres, considered the world's preeminent guitar-maker. Guitar enthusiasts, take note: a visit here culminates with the chance to play some of the instruments.

Perfect for rainy days, regular concerts, including final degree performances, are often free. Musical children will love the family-friendly workshops, which cover everything from making your own ukelele to introducing the sounds of Indonesian gamelan and Korean janggu.

Every Sunday (except in August and the first half of September), visitors can join a free guided tour.

Did You Know?

The Egyptian Museum has a substantial collection of fertility figures engaged in sexual activity.

Museu Egipci de Barcelona

⑨G4 **🏠Carrer de València 284** **🚇Passeig de Gràcia** **🕐10am-2pm & 4-8pm Mon-Fri (no lunch break Jun-Sep), 10am-8pm Sat, 10am-2pm Sun** **🌐museuegipci.com**

This private collection of Ancient Egyptian art is one of the finest in the world, with more than 1,000 artifacts dating back several millennia. The collection begins with the Egyptians pharaohs, who were worshipped as gods.

One of the most popular sections features sarcophagi, which range from early, simply decorated terracotta versions to huge, elaborately painted caskets. The sarcophagi are displayed with canopic jars, used to hold the intestines of mummified bodies. These jars were often decorated with the symbols of the four sons of Horus, who were believed to protect the contents.

There is also an excellent collection of intricate jewellery, pottery, weapons and even an Egyptian bed. Note that the information available in English is limited, so it is worth downloading the museum's own app (available on the website). The museum offers an extensive range of activities, from sleepovers, where kids camp among the exhibits, to breakfast talks.

↑ Viewing a glass-encased sarcophagus at the Museu Egipci de Barcelona

STAY

Hotel Constanza
This boutique hotel has rooms in soothing Mediterranean shades, some with balconies.

⑨H5 **🏠Calle Bruc 33** **🌐hotelconstanza.com**

€€€

Cotton House Hotel
A plush 5-star hotel offering elegant white-on-white "cotton rooms", sumptuous suites filled with antiques and a rooftop plunge pool.

⑨H5 **🏠Gran Via de les Corts Catalanes 670** **🌐hotelcottonhouse.com**

€€€

A SHORT WALK
QUADRAT D'OR

Distance 1.5 km (1 mile) **Nearest metro**
Passeig de Gràcia, Diagonal **Time** 25 minutes

The hundred or so city blocks centering on the Passeig de Gràcia are known as the Quadrat d'Or, "Golden Square", because they contain so many of Barcelona's best Modernista buildings *(p84)*. This was the area within the Eixample favoured by the wealthy bourgeoisie, who embraced the new artistic and architectural style with enthusiasm. Take a stroll through the area to discover beautiful private residences, as well as ornamented commercial buildings. Most remarkable is the Illa de la Discòrdia, a single block with houses by Modernisme's most illustrious exponents. Many interiors can be visited, revealing a feast of stained glass, ceramics and ironwork.

Diagonal metro

CARRER DE PROVENÇA

*The Eixample's main avenue, **Passeig de Gràcia** is a showcase of highly original buildings and smart shops.*

CARRER DE MALLORCA

PASSEIG DE GRÀCIA

*Topped by Tàpies' sculpture Cloud and Chair, the **Fundació Antoni Tàpies** (p117) was designed by Domènech i Montaner in 1879.*

CARRER DE VALÈNCIA

↑ Looking through a stained-glass door at Casa Lleó Morera

Casa Amatller

*In the **Illa de la Discòrdia**, three of Barcelona's most famous Modernista houses vie for attention (p116). All were created between 1900 and 1910.*

Museu del Perfum

Casa Ramon Mulleras

START

Casa Lleó Morera

*Gaudí's **Casa Batlló** (p112)*

Passeig de Gràcia metro

```
0 metres        100   N
0 yards         100   ↗
```

The **Palau Baró de Quadras** was designed by Puig i Cadafalch in 1904. The façade, in Neo-Gothic style, is highly ornate and covered with distinctive sculptures.

Gaudí put all his architectural daring into **La Pedrera** (p114). The result is a remarkable wave-like façade and a roofscape of abstract chimneys and vents.

Locator Map
For more detail see p104

AVINGUDA DIAGONAL

CARRER DE PAU CLARIS

CARRER DE PROVENÇA

Built in red brick with carved-stone ornamentation, **Casa Terrades** was built in 1905 by Puig i Cadafalch (p119). It echoes the Gothic buildings of northern Europe, and was the architect's largest work.

Did You Know?

Poet Pere Gimferrer christened La Pedrera as "the garden of warriors" because of its chimneys.

FINISH

CARRER DE MALLORCA

Casa Thomas

CARRER DE VALÈNCIA

CARRER DE ROGER DE LLÚRIA

CARRER DEL BRUC

Palau Ramon de Montaner

CARRER D'ARAGÓ

↑ Sculpted chimneys on the roof of Gaudí's La Pedrera, a dramatic apartment building

MONTJUÏC

There was probably a Celtiberian settlement on this 185-m- (607-ft-) high hill before the Romans built a temple to Jupiter here, on what they called Mons Jovis (the Hill of Jove), which may have given Montjuïc its name. Another theory suggests that the hill was once home to a Jewish cemetery and that the name Montjuïc developed from it being called Mount of the Jews.

Naturally wooded, the slopes of Montjuïc were for years used to grow food and graze cattle to feed the Old Town. The absence of a water supply meant that there were few buildings on Montjuïc until a castle was erected on the top in 1640. This garrison famously shelled parts of Barcelona in 1842 to end an insurgency against Isabella II. The hill finally came into its own as the site of the 1929 International Exhibition. With great energy and flair, buildings were erected all over the north side, with the grand Avinguda de la Reina Maria Cristina, lined with huge exhibition halls, leading onto the base of the hill from the Plaça d'Espanya. One of these buildings was a stadium intended to host an alternative 1936 Olympics, in opposition to the Nazi-hosted competition in Berlin, but the event was cancelled on the outbreak of the Spanish Civil War. It seems fitting, then, that the last great surge of building on Montjuïc was for the 1992 Olympic Games, which left Barcelona with world-class sports facilities.

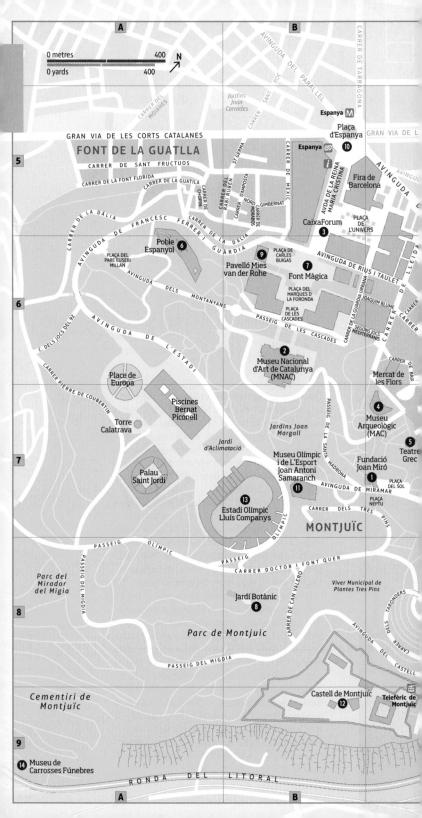

MONTJUÏC

Must Sees
① Fundació Joan Miró
② Museu Nacional d'Art de Catalunya

Experience More
③ CaixaForum
④ Museu d'Arqueologia de Catalunya (MAC)
⑤ Teatre Grec
⑥ Poble Espanyol
⑦ Font Màgica
⑧ Jardí Botànic
⑨ Pavelló Mies van der Rohe
⑩ Plaça d'Espanya
⑪ Museu Olímpic i de L'Esport Joan Antoni Samaranch

⑫ Castell de Montjuïc
⑬ Estadi Olímpic Lluís Companys
⑭ Museu de Carrosses Fúnebres

Eat
① Pakta
② Quimet i Quimet
③ Malamén

Drink
④ Cerveceriá Jazz
⑤ Bar Calders
⑥ Bodega Saltó

Stay
⑦ Hotel Miramar Barcelona
⑧ Casa Vaganto

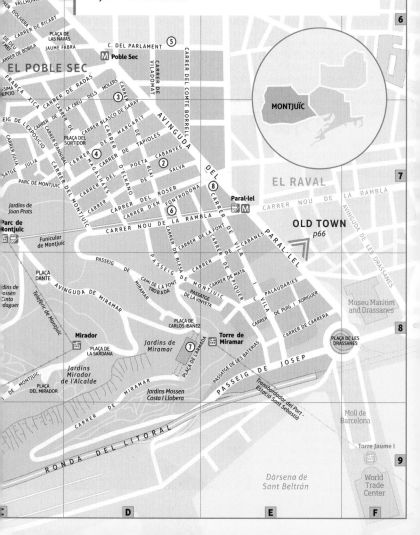

❶ 🐾 🐾 🍴 🛍️

FUNDACIÓ JOAN MIRÓ

📍 C7 🏛️ Parc de Montjuïc 🚌 150 🚠 To Montjuïc 🕐 Apr-Oct: 10am-8pm Tue, Wed, Fri & Sat, 10am-9:30pm Thu, 10am-6pm Sun; Nov-Mar: 10am-6pm Tue-Sat, 10am-3pm Sun & public hols 🚫 1, 6 & 19-25 Jan, 25 & 26 Dec 🌐 fmirobcn.org

Established in 1975 by the artist himself, the Fundació Joan Miró contains an enormous permanent collection of over 14,000 pieces, most of which were donated from Miró's private collection. The works include Miró's own as well as other pieces of contemporary art.

Designed by architect Josep Lluís Sert, the stark, white building that houses the foundation is a remarkable Rationalist construction arranged around courtyards and drenched with natural light that pours in through angled skylights. Guided tours of the building take place on the first Sunday of each month, in English, Spanish or Catalan.

Miró himself donated his own works, and some of the best pieces on display include his Barcelona Series (1939–44), a set of 50 black-and-white lithographs, and Chapel of Sant Joan d'Horta, painted in 1917 in the Catalan town which features prominently in Miró's early work.

The foundation also has an exquisite collection of artworks by other celebrated artists, including Alexander Calder and Lola Fernández Jiménez. When Miró first conceived of the museum, he wanted to create a space in which young artists could experiment, and the Espai 13 gallery showcases the work of emerging artists. The foundation also hosts blockbuster exhibitions, which attract such huge crowds that the queues snake down the hill.

TOP 5 UNMISSABLE WORKS

Chapel of Sant Joan d'Horta (1917)
An early landscape, in vivid Fauvist colours.

Painting (The White Glove) (1925)
A poetic, abstract work influenced by the Surrealist movement.

Morning Star (1940)
Part of the celebrated Constellations series.

Poem (III) (1968)
Miró claimed to "paint colours like words that shape poems".

Tapestry of the Foundation (1979)
This tapestry of a woman dancing under the moon and stars was created for this space.

JOAN MIRÓ

Joan Miró (1893-1983) started taking art classes when he was seven years old and moved to La Llotja's art school in 1907. From 1919, he spent much time in Paris, where he honed his own unique artistic language, displayed in remarkable paintings like *Man and Woman in Front of a Pile of Excrement* (1935) – Miró's reaction to the simmering violence that would erupt in the Spanish Civil War. An admirer of Catalan art and Modernisme, Miró invented and developed a Surrealistic style, with exuberant colours and fantastical forms.

> GREAT VIEW
> ### Jardí de les Escultures
>
> After a visit through the gallery step into the small adjacent sculpture garden, where you'll find wonderful panoramic views of the city from shaded picnic benches. It's a perfect place to recalibrate.

↑ The stark, white façade of the Fundació Joan Miró, designed by Josep Lluís Sert

↑ Admiring the vibrant streaks of colour in the paintings of Joan Miró

2 🎟️ 🍴 🖥️ 🛍️

MUSEU NACIONAL D'ART DE CATALUNYA

📍B6 🏛️Parc de Montjuïc, Palau Nacional 🚇Espanya 🚌150 🕐May–Sep: 10am–8pm Tue–Sat, 10am–3pm Sun; Oct–Apr: 10am–6pm Tue–Sat, 10am–3pm Sun 📅1 Jan, 1 May, 25 Dec 🌐museunacional.cat

The austere Palau Nacional was built for the 1929 International Exhibition, but since 1934 it has housed the city's most important art collection. The artworks span 1,000 years, and include paintings, sculpture, furniture, photographs, drawings, prints and coins.

With its origins in the 19th century and the Renaixença's focus on Catalonia's artistic heritage, the museum's collection of Catalan art grew from two separate institutions: the Museu Provincial d'Antiguitats (Provincial Museum of Antiquities, established in 1880) and the Museu Municipal de Belles Arts (Municipal Museum of Fine Arts, inaugurated in 1891). These two collections were moved to the exquisite Palau Nacional between 1934 and 1942. During the rest of the 20th century the museum was expanded to include other collections, from Romanesque to modern art. Today the museum hosts regular major exhibitions of primarily Catalan artists, but also Spanish and European.

Tickets are valid for two days, so there's no need to attempt to see everything in one trip. The museum's website has a handy "create your own itinerary" function, to help you make the most of your visit.

Waterfalls cascading below the must-visit Museu Nacional d'Art de Catalunya ↑

Must See

Coins

The numismatic collection contains more than 100,000 coins, the earliest dating back as far as the 6th century BC.

Romanesque Collection

▷ The museum's excellent display of Romanesque items centres on a series of magnificent 12th-century frescoes. The most remarkable are the wall paintings from Sant Climent de Taüll and La Seu d'Urgell. The displays were specially designed to recall the remote Pyrenean churches from which the frescoes came.

Gothic Collection

The superb Gothic collection includes notable works by the 15th-century Catalan artists Bernat Martorell, Lluís Dalmau and Jaume Huguet. These impressive, often richly gilded works reflect Catalonia's growing wealth and power in this era.

The Cambó Bequest

▷ The Cambó Bequest, donated by the collector and politician Francesc Cambó, includes works by El Greco, Zurbarán and Velázquez. Paired with paintings on permanent loan from Madrid's Thyssen-Bornemisza collection, the bequest ensures that the museum has an impressive Renaissance and Baroque collection.

Modernisme and Noucentisme

◁ The museum's remarkable selection of 19th- and early 20th-century artworks and decorative objects includes beautiful curving furniture designs by Gaudí for the Casa Batlló. Also in the collection is the famous painting by Ramon Casas of himself and Pere Romeu on a tandem, which once hung in the Els 4 Gats tavern.

Photography Collection

The photography collection runs the gamut from early 19th-century portraits to gritty photojournalism from the Spanish Civil War.

CATALONIA'S RENAIXENÇA

Just as the wealth of the 14th century inspired Catalonia's first flowering, so the wealth from industry in the 19th century inspired the Renaixença, a renaissance of Catalan language and culture (similar to the Galician Rexurdimento). Its literary rallying points were Bonaventura Aribau's *Oda a la patria*, published in 1833, and the poems of a young monk, Jacint Verdaguer, who won prizes in the revived Jocs Florals poetry competitions. The Catalan language was finally standardized in the early 20th century.

131

EXPERIENCE MORE

CaixaForum

🅱️ B5 📍 Avinguda de Francesc Ferrer i Guàrdia 6–8, Montjuïc 📞 93 476 86 00 🚇 Espanya 🚌 13, 150 🕐 10am–8pm daily (to 11pm Wed Jul–Aug) 🚫 1 & 6 Jan, 25 Dec 🌐 caixaforum.es

Barcelona grows ever-stronger in the field of contemporary art and this intriguing exhibition centre only enhances its reputation. The foundation's collection of 700 works by Spanish and international artists is housed in the Antiga Fàbrica Casaramona, a beautifully restored textile mill built in the early 20th century in the Modernista style.

The mill was built by Josep Puig i Cadafalch after he had completed the Casa de les Punxes. Opened in 1911, it was intended to be a model factory – light, clean and airy – but had only a short working life before the business closed down in 1920. At this point the building became a storehouse and, after the Civil War, stables for police horses.

Reclaimed as a gallery space in 2002, there are a series of galleries dedicated to temporary displays (often major international touring exhibitions), plus a permanent collection of contemporary art. A free app provides visitors with an audio guide of the items on display. Look out for family workshops, concerts, talks, film screenings and other cultural events – many of which are free. Also, don't miss the roof terrace, which offers great views of the city.

Museu d'Arqueologia de Catalunya (MAC)

🅲 C7 📍 Passeig de Santa Madrona 39–41 🚇 Espanya, Poble Sec 🕐 9:30am–7pm Tue–Sat, 10am–2:30pm Sun & public hols 🚫 1 Jan, 25 & 26 Dec 🌐 mac.cat

Housed in the 1929 Palace of Graphic Arts, this fascinating archaeology museum brims with artifacts from prehistory to the Visigothic period

(AD 415–711). The mysterious *talayots* (Bronze Age megaliths) from the Balearics are described here, and there are beautiful collections of Hellenic Mallorcan jewellery and Iberian silver treasures. Among the highlights of the collection is the Dama d'Eivissa ("The Lady of Ibiza"), a remarkable 4th-century sculpture of an elaborately dressed goddess, and the startling 2nd-century Roman fertility symbol, Priapus of Hostafrancs.

The museum has a superb collection of artifacts gathered from the Greco-Roman town of Empúries (*p186*), once the most important Greek colony on the entire Spanish peninsula. The displays include exquisite mosaics, everyday items such as oil lamps and amphorae, and several statues, including a copy of the famous Asclepius (the original remains in situ). Finally, the collection has a horde of ornate, gem-encrusted Visigothic jewellery, belt buckles, helmets

GREAT VIEW
Cable Car

Barcelona has many great viewpoints, but none quite as vertiginous as Montjuïc's cable car. It runs from just below the castle and delivers a citywide panorama as it glides above manicured gardens.

and armour. In addition to this permanent collection, there are temporary exhibits.

Written information in English can be sparse throughout the museum; instead, pick up the excellent English-language audio guide.

↑ The Teatre Grec, a renowned festival venue nestled amid lovely gardens

---

5

Teatre Grec

🄌 C7 🄰 Parc de Montjuïc
🄑 Poble Sec, then 55 bus
🄒 Dawn to dusk daily (only ticket holders permitted during the El Grec Festival)
🅆 lameva.barcelona.cat/grec/en

This remarkable outdoor amphitheatre is hidden away amid

greenery at the foot of Montjuïc. Originally a quarry, it was converted into an open-air theatre in 1929 by Catalan architects Ramon Revento and Nicolau Maria Rubió i Tudurí, when Montjuïc was remodelled as part of the International Exhibition. This is easily one of the most atmospheric venues in the city, set amid extensive gardens, with groves of orange trees, pretty pavilions and a series of terraces and viewing points that frame beautiful views of the gardens themselves and the city beyond. It is said to have been inspired by the ancient Greek theatre at Epidaurus, and it is the epicentre of Barcelona's biggest performing arts festival.

Once a year, in late June and all of July, the theatre steps up its game for the Festival Grec. The popular arts festival has been held at the amphitheatre since 1976, when the venue was taken over by Barcelona's city council. A varied programme of events takes place and a buzzing open-air bar and restaurant pop up in the gardens during the festival.

←

The CaixaForum, a modern art gallery, dramatically lit up at night

---

EAT

Pakta
Head here for Michelin-starred Nikkei (Peruvian and Japanese fusion) cuisine, by Albert Adrià, younger brother of super-chef Ferran.

🄌 C6 🄰 Carrer de Lleida 5 🅆 elbarri.com

€€€

Quimet i Quimet
The *montaditos* (tapas mounted on bread) at this diminutive bar are quite possibly the best in the city.

🄌 D7 🄰 Carrer del Poeta Cabanyes 25 🅆 quimetquimet.com

€€€

Malamén
Experimental dishes based on local cuisine are served here, in tapas or regular-sized options.

🄌 D6 🄰 Carrer de Blai 53 🅆 malamen.es

€€€

↑ Wandering the picturesque streets of Poble Espanyol, overlooked by balconies

STAY

Hotel Miramar Barcelona

Ask for a room with a sea view at this gorgeously swanky hotel standing in the gardens of Montjuïc.

📍D8 🏠Plaça de Carlos Ibáñez 3 🌐hotelmiramarbarcelona.com

€€€

Casa Vaganto

Find great design and cosy rooms at this sanctuary in the city.

📍E7 🏠Carrer d'En Fontrodona 1 🌐vagantohotel.com

€€€

6

Poble Espanyol

📍A6 🏠Avinguda Francesc Ferrer i Guàrdia 🚇Espanya 🕐9am–8pm Mon, 9am–midnight Tue–Thu & Sun, 9am–3am Fri, 9am–4am Sat 🌐poble-espanyol.com

The idea behind the Poble Espanyol (Spanish Village) was to illustrate and display local Spanish architectural styles and crafts. It was laid out for the 1929 International Exhibition, but has proved to be enduringly popular and now attracts well over a million visitors a year. More than 100 buildings, streets and squares from across Spain have been re-created – from whitewashed Andalusian homes to arcaded Castilian squares, Catalan villages to Basque farmhouses. Replicas of the towers in the walled city of Ávila in central Spain form the impressive main entrance.

Resident artisans produce crafts, including hand-blown glass, Toledo damascene, leather goods and musical instruments. There is plenty more to entertain visitors, including restaurants, bars, a flamenco show, a museum of modern art and a programme of craft and music workshops.

7

Font Màgica

📍B6 🏠Plaça de Carles Buïgas 🚇Espanya 🕐Nov–Jan 6 & Mar: 8–9pm Thu–Sat; Apr, May & Oct: 9–10pm Thu–Sat; Jun–Sep: 9:30pm–10:30pm Wed–Sun 🚫7 Jan–Feb

This marvel of engineering was built by Carles Buïgas (1898–1979) for the International Exhibition. The Art Deco fountain shoots jets of multicoloured water to music in exuberant sound-and-light shows. Themes vary, but the show often culminates with Montserrat Caballé and Freddie Mercury's popular duet "Barcelona", performed at the 1992 Olympics.

The four columns behind the Font Màgica were originally erected by Modernista architect Puig i Cadafalch at the turn of the 20th century. Designed to represent the stripes on the Catalan coat-of-arms, they were destroyed in 1928 as part of a ban on Catalan symbols. Now rebuilt, they are once again a potent symbol of Catalan pride.

8

Jardí Botànic

📍B8 🏠Parc de Montjuïc 📞932 56 41 60 🚇Espanya 🕐Apr–May & Sep: 10am–7pm daily; Jun–Aug: 10am–8pm daily; Oct–Mar: 10am–6pm daily 🚫1 Jan, 1 May, 24 Jun, 25 Dec

Set on a sloping hill in Montjuïc Park, Barcelona's

Did You Know?

The Poble Espanyol was built in just 13 months, for the 1929 International Exhibition.

botanic garden offers an insight into the flora of the Mediterranean and beyond. You won't find lush tropical plants here, rather this botanic garden is home to the types of plants that can survive Barcelona's hot, dry Mediterranean summers.

A walk around the grounds takes you through gardens reminiscent of the *matollar* scrubland that covers much of Catalonia. Native species are well represented, as well as plants from places around the world with a similar climate. Try to visit in spring, when most of the garden is abloom with bright neons and muted pastels; the plants are least impressive in summer, when only those with the deepest roots can find water to flower.

9

Pavelló Mies van der Rohe

B6 **Avinguda Francesc Ferrer i Guàrdia 7** **Espanya** **50** **Summer: 10am-8pm daily; winter: 10am-6pm daily** **1 Jan, 25 Dec** **miesbcn.com**

The modern, simple lines of the German Pavilion must have shocked visitors to the International Exhibition. The pavilion was designed by Ludwig Mies van der Rohe, director of the avant-garde Bauhaus school, and his close collaborator Lilly Reich. The pavilion was characterized by fluid, glassy spaces, in which the boundaries between inside and outside were blurred, and made use of materials like marble and onyx. This was enhanced by highly polished façades and extensive use of tinted glass. Two pools are set into the pavilion surroundings, one of which is overlooked by a bronze reproduction of the statue *Alba* (Dawn) by Georg Kolbe. Unlike other pavilions at the exhibition, this one was conceived as a place of rest and tranquillity for visitors rather than as a gallery. Nothing was displayed within its walls except the steel-and-leather Barcelona Chair. The original was made of ivory-coloured pigskin, and was designed specifically for the Spanish royal family as they made their way through the exhibition's pavilions and display spaces. The building was intended to be a temporary structure and was dismantled after the exhibition, but an exact replica was painstakingly rebuilt using the same materials in the 1980s, for the centenary of the designer's birth.

> **PICTURE PERFECT**
> **Dawn Chorus**
>
> The best place to get the perfect shot of *Alba* is to stand at the opposite end of the pool, where you can get a picture of the statue reflected not just in the water, but also in the glass façade to the left.

← The stark, soothing interior of the Pavelló Mies van der Rohe

Spanish architectural styles displayed in Poble Espanyol

10

Plaça d'Espanya

◉ B5 ⊞ Gran Via de les
Corts Catalanes ⊞ Espanya

At the centre of this busy
junction is an impressive
fountain by Josep Maria Jujol,
one of Gaudí's most faithful
collaborators. The huge 1899
bullring to one side, by August
Font i Carreras, features a
dazzling red-brick façade. It
has been converted into Las
Arenas, a shopping centre with
an observation deck on the
roof where you can enjoy
fantastic views of Montjuïc.
On the Montjuïc side the
Avinguda de la Reina Maria
Cristina is flanked by two campaniles modelled on the bell
towers of St Mark's in Venice
and built for the 1929
International Exhibition.

11

Museu Olímpic i de
L'Esport Joan Antoni
Samaranch

◉ B7 ⊞ Avinguda de
l'Estadi 60 ◷ Apr-Sep:
10am-8pm Tue-Sat, 10am-
2:30pm Sun; Oct-Mar: 10am-
6pm Tue-Sat, 10am-2:30pm
Sun ⊞ museuolimpic
bcn.cat

This museum pays homage to
the 1992 Olympic Games held

in Barcelona. Exhibits cover
the history of the modern
Olympic Games, and have a
marvellous collection of mem-
orabilia, including items from
the personal collection of Juan
Antonio Samaranch, former
President of the International
Olympic Committee, to whom
the museum is dedicated.

12

Castell de Montjuïc

◉ B9 ⊞ Parc de Montjuïc
☎ 93 256 44 40 ⊞ Paral·lel,
then funicular & cable car
🚌 150 from Plaça Espanya
◷ Mar-Oct: 10am-8pm; Nov-
Feb: 10am-6pm

Crowning the very summit of
Montjuïc is an 18th-century

HIDDEN GEM
Woodland Café

Evenings get groovy
with flamenco and
rumba nights at café La
Caseta del Migdia
(*lacaseta.org*) behind
Castell de Montjuïc.
Glorious harbour views
are a bonus.

---

castle with spectacular views
over the entire city and a vast
stretch of the coastline. The
first fortress here was built in
1640, and became the site of
numerous battles during the
War of the Spanish Succession
in the early 1700s. After the
success of Felipe V, Montjuïc
fortress was rebuilt by the
Bourbon rulers in order to
ensure that the local populace
was kept under control. It
became infamous as a prison
and torture centre, a role it
continued to play until after
the Civil War. Notable Catalan
leaders were imprisoned and
executed here in the after-
math of the Spanish Civil War,
including Lluís Companys.

The castle contained a
military museum for several
decades, but when it was
formally restored to the
Catalan authorities by the
Spanish government in 2008,
it was decided that the
military museum be turned
into a centre dedicated to
peace. Exhibits describe the
development of Montjuïc and
the castle's turbulent history.
There's a café with a terrace
on the Pati d'Armes and, in
summer, an outdoor cinema in
the gardens.

← Plaça d'Espanya and the twin campaniles of Avinguda de la Reina Maria Cristina

13 🖊 🖼 🏛

Estadi Olímpic Lluís Companys

📍 B7 🚪 Passeig Olímpic 📞 93 426 20 89 🚇 Espanya, Poble Sec 🚌 55 ⏰ Museum: Apr-Sep: 10am-8pm Tue-Sat, 10am-2pm Sun; Oct-Mar: 10am-6pm Tue-Sat, 10am-2pm Sun 📅 1 Jan, 1 May, 25 & 26 Dec

This stadium – the centrepiece of the so-called Anella Olímpica (Olympic Ring) of sports facilities erected for the 1992 Olympics – was originally built in 1929 for the International Exhibition. It was remodelled to host the Olímpiada Popular in 1936. This event (conceived as a protest against the Olympics being held in Berlin under Hitler) never took place due to the outbreak of the Spanish Civil War. However, the stadium got its chance to shine in the 1992 Olympics, for which it was modernized, although the original façade was preserved.

Next door is the modern Museu Olímpic i de l'Esport, and nearby are the steel-and-glass Palau Sant Jordi stadium, Barcelona's biggest concert venue; the Piscines Picornell, which includes a gym and indoor and outdoor swimming pools; and the diving pools used in the Olympics. These are open in summer and offer superb views over the city.

14

Museu de Carrosses Fúnebres

📍 A9 🚪 Carrer de la Mare de Déu de Port 56 📞 934 84 19 20 ⏰ 10am-2pm Sat & Sun

Within Monjuïc Cemetery is this unusual, mildly macabre museum, dedicated to the history of funeral processions. Visitors are taken downstairs to a permanent collection of funeral carriages and coaches that date back to the 18th century. Twentieth-century motor hearses are also included, with eerie mannequins in period dress keeping watch over the entire collection.

Entry is free, but the best time to visit is on the annual La Nit dels Museus festival, when you can visit after dark for added chills.

← An ornate hearse, one of the exhibits at the Museu de Carrosses Fúnebres

DRINK

Cervecería Jazz
One of the first bars in the city to specialize in craft beer, this joint also does a strong line of hamburgers - and, of course, jazz.

📍 D7 🚪 Carrer de Margarit 43 🌐 cerveceriajazz.com

Bar Calders
A decent selection of wine (and tapas) is available at this Sant Antoni favourite, which has tables outside on a pedestrianized street.

📍 D6 🚪 Carrer del Parlament 25 📞 933 29 93 49

Bodega Saltó
An eccentric little bar, with barrels, papier-mâché models and mannequins on the walls. A stage sees all manner of live acts.

📍 D7 🚪 Carrer del Blesa 36 🌐 bodegasalto.net

A SHORT WALK
MONTJUÏC

Distance 3 km (2 miles) **Nearest metro**
Espanya **Time** 45 minutes

Set high on a hill, Montjuïc is a spectacular vantage point
from which to view the city. On a walk through the area,
you'll find a wealth of art galleries and museums, an
amusement park and an open-air theatre. The most
interesting buildings lie around the Palau Nacional, where
Europe's greatest Romanesque art
collection is housed. Montjuïc is
approached from the Plaça
d'Espanya between brick pillars
based on the campanile of St Mark's
in Venice, which give a foretaste of
the eclecticism of building styles.
The Poble Espanyol illustrates the
traditional architecture of Spain's
regions, while the Fundació Joan
Miró is boldly modern.

*A steel, glass, stone and
onyx pavilion,* **Pavelló Mies
van der Rohe** *was built in
the Bauhaus style as the
German contribution to the
1929 International
Exhibition (p135).*

START

AVINGUDA DE FRANCESC FERRER I GUARDIA

*Containing replicas of
buildings from many
regions, the* **Poble
Espanyol** *provides a
fascinating glimpse
of vernacular
styles (p134).*

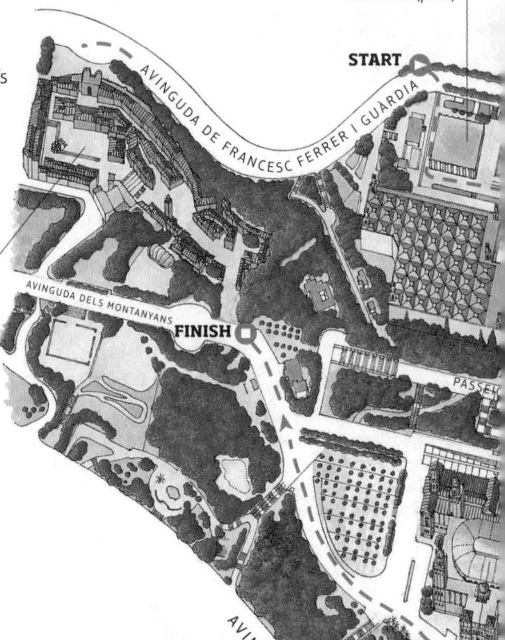

AVINGUDA DELS MONTANYANS

FINISH

PASSEIG

| 0 metres | 100 |
| 0 yards | 100 |

N

AVINGUDA DE L'ESTADI

*Displayed in the Palau
Nacional, the* **Museu
Nacional d'Art de
Catalunya (MNAC)**
*includes Europe's
finest collection of
early medieval
frescoes (p130).*

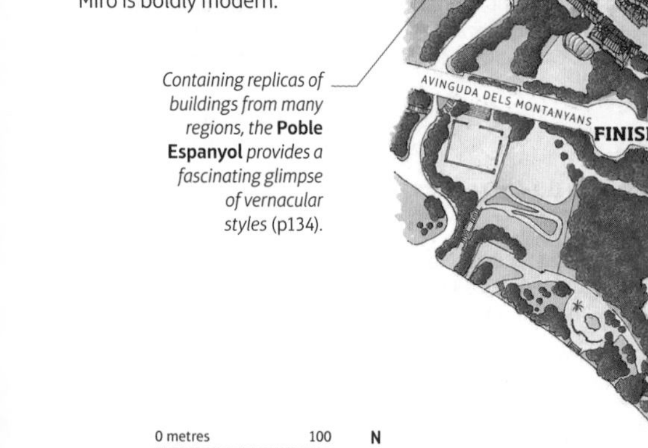

↑ Walking under an arch on a street
   in the Poble Espanyol

↑ People watching the dramatic Font Màgica, in front of the MNAC

Locator Map
For more detail see p126

Fountains and cascades descend in terraces from the Palau Nacional. Below them is the **Font Màgica** (p134). This marvel of engineering was built for the 1929 International Exhibition.

RIUS I TAULET

CARRER DE LA GUARDIA URBANA

CARRER DE LLEIDA

ASCADES

PASSEIG DE LA SANTA MADRONA

PASSEIG DE LA SANTA MADRONA

PASSEIG DE LA SANTA MADRONA

AVINGUDA DE MIRAMAR

Did You Know?

The Ibero-American Exposition was held in Seville at the same time as Barcelona's Exhibition.

Mercat de les Flors *theatre*

The **Museu d'Arqueologia de Catalunya (MAC)** *displays important finds from prehistoric cultures in Catalonia and the Balearic Islands (p132).*

Teatre Grec *is an open-air theatre set among gardens.*

Miró created the **Fundació Joan Miró** *as a centre for the study of modern art (p128). In addition to Miró's works in various media, the modern building by Josep Lluís Sert is of architectural interest.*

The Montjuïc branch of the **Museu Etnològic i de Cultures del Món** *displays artifacts from Oceania, Africa, Asia and Latin America.*

Sunset views from El Carmel bunker

BEYOND THE CENTRE

A period of radical redevelopment of Barcelona's outskirts in the late 1980s and 1990s gave it a wealth of new buildings, parks and squares and restored a trove of Modernista buildings. The city's main station, Sants, was rebuilt and the neighbouring Parc de l'Espanya Industrial and Parc de Joan Miró were created containing lakes, modern sculpture and futuristic architecture. In the west of the city, where the streets start to climb steeply, the historic royal palace and monastery of Pedralbes, plus Gaudí's famous Park Güell were restored, and the Torre de Collserola, built for the 1992 Olympics, gave *barcelonins* the chance to see it all from above.

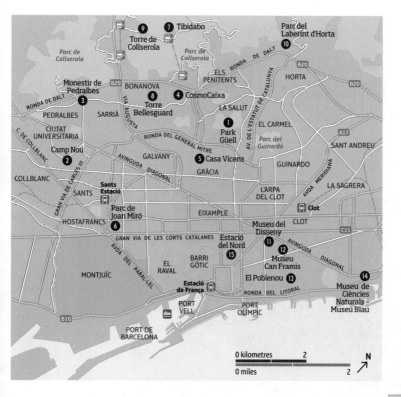

1 🖈 Ⓜ

PARK GÜELL

🏠 Carrer d'Olot 7, Vallcarca Ⓜ Lesseps, Vallcarca 🚌 24, 32, 92, H6 🕐 Park Güell: Mar: 8am-7pm daily; Apr, Sep & Oct: 8am-8:30pm daily; May-Aug: 8am-9:30pm daily; Nov-Feb: 8am-6:30pm daily (last adm: 1 hr before closing; timed tickets only); Casa Museu Gaudí: Apr-Sep: 9am-8pm daily; Oct-Mar: 10am-6pm daily 🚫 Casa Museu Gaudí: 1 Jan 🕸 Park Güell: parkguell.cat; Casa Museu Gaudí: casamuseugaudi.org

A UNESCO World Heritage Site, Park Güell is Antoni Gaudí's most colourful creation. Conceived as a garden city, but never completed, it is now a stunning park that spills down Carmel Hill. Several of Gaudí's creations survive, including a pair of fairy-tale pavilions, a tiled salamander and the world's longest bench.

Gaudí was commissioned in the 1890s by Count Eusebi Güell to design a garden city on 20 hectares (50 acres) of his family estate, but the planned public buildings and 60 houses didn't come to fruition. What we see today was completed between 1910 and 1914, and the park opened in 1922. The Monumental Area, home to most of Gaudí's surviving creations, requires a ticket, but the green expanses around the edge of this area are free to explore.

The Room of a Hundred Columns is a cavernous hall of 84 crooked pillars; it was intended as the marketplace for the estate. Above it is the Gran Plaça Circular, an open space with a snaking balcony of coloured mosaics that offers stunning views of the city.

Two pavilions at the entry are by Gaudí, but the Casa Museu Gaudí, a gingerbread-style house where Gaudí lived from 1906 to 1926, was built by Francesc Berenguer.

📷 PICTURE PERFECT
Double Shot

The Park Güell gives you two options for that ultimate Barcelona photograph: the mosaic-covered salamander that has become the park's emblem and the views from the Gran Plaça Circular.

1

1. The two fairy-tale-like gatehouses have intricately tiled exteriors. Inside one is a museum with displays outlining the park's history.

2. The Casa-Museu Gaudí has a beautiful garden with architectural features, such as these mosaics.

3. At the top of the stairs to the Gran Plaça Circular is Gaudí's salamander.

2

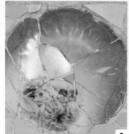

3

↑ The Gran Plaça Circular, sitting on top of the Room of a Hundred Columns

99,354
The seating capacity of the stadium.

② ⚽ Ⓜ

CAMP NOU

📍 Carrer d'Aristides Maillol 🚇 Maria Cristina, Collblanc 🕐 Mid-Apr–mid-Oct, Christmas & Easter hols: 9:30am–7:30pm daily; mid-Oct–mid-Apr: 10am–6:30pm Mon–Sat, 10am–2:30pm Sun; reduced hours on public hols & match days 🚫 1 Jan, 25 Dec 🌐 fcbarcelona.cat

Camp Nou, Europe's largest football stadium, is home to the city's famous football club, Barcelona FC (known locally as Barça). Founded in 1899, it is one of the world's richest soccer clubs, and has more than 140,000 members.

Blau-grana (blue-burgundy), the colours of Barça's strip, hold an important place in the city's heart. The club's flags were used as an expression of local nationalist feelings during the Franco dictatorship, when the Catalan flag was banned.

The stadium is a magnificent, sweeping structure, built in 1957 to a design by Francesc Mitjans and Josep Soteras. An extension was added in 1982 and it can now comfortably seat nearly 100,000 fans.

The Barça Stadium Tour includes a visit to the club's popular museum, where Barcelona FC's many trophies are displayed. This is a glossy interactive experience, with touch-screen panels detailing the club's history and their many victories. After exploring the museum, visitors are taken on a tour of the stadium – from the changing rooms to the impossibly green pitch, the site of so many hotly contested matches.

↑ The László Kubala memorial in front of the stadium

BARCELONA VS REAL MADRID

"Més que un club" ("More than a club") is the motto of Barcelona FC. More than anything else it has been a symbol of the struggle of Catalan nationalism against the central government in Madrid.

To fail to win La Liga Santander is one thing; to come in behind Real Madrid is a disaster. Each season the big question is which of the two teams will win the title. In a memorable episode in 1941, Barça won 3–0 at home. At the return match in Madrid, the crowd was so hostile that the police and referee "advised" Barça to prevent trouble. Demoralized by the intimidation, they lost 11–1.

↑ An aerial view of Camp Nou, packed with fans on a match day

← Walking down the colourful tunnel that takes players to the pitch

→ Admiring trophies in the Barça museum at Camp Nou

3

MONESTIR DE PEDRALBES

🏠 Baixada del Monestir 9 ☎ 932 56 34 34 🚇 Reina Elisenda ⏰ Apr-Sep: 10am-2pm Tue-Fri, 10am-7pm Sat, 10am-8pm Sun; Oct-Mar: 10am-2pm Tue-Fri, 10am-5pm Sat & Sun by appt 🚫 1 Jan, 1 May, 24 Jun, 25 Dec 🌐 monestirpedralbes.bcn.cat

Founded in 1326 by Elisenda de Montcada, fourth wife of Jaume II of Catalonia and Aragón, the monastery was home to the nuns of the Order of St Clare until 1983. Today, the monastery's church and cloister are considered to be an exemplar of Catalan Gothic architecture.

Approached through an ancient arch, the lovely monastery of Pedralbes retains the air of an enclosed community. This ambience is heightened by its well-preserved furnished kitchens, cells, infirmary and refectory. The nuns of the Order of St Clare moved to an adjoining property in 1983, when the monastery was opened to the public. The alabaster tomb of Elisenda de Montcada lies in the wall between church and cloister. On the church side, her effigy is dressed in royal robes; on the other, in a nun's habit.

The monastery is built around a three-storey cloister. Numerous works of art, as well as liturgical ornaments and pottery, are on display here. The Capella (chapel) de Sant Miquel has murals of the Passion and the Life of the Virgin, both painted by Ferrer Bassa in 1346. A medieval apothecary garden features medicinal herbs and other plants once used in the monastery's infirmary.

↑ Flowering plants framing the ancient walls of the well-preserved Monestir de Pedralbes

💬 INSIDER TIP
Capella de Sant Miquel

Ferrar Bassa's murals in the quiet Capella de Sant Miquel depict the Passion and the Life of the Virgin in three pictorial strips running from left to right. On the upper level are paintings of the saints.

← Admiring the Gothic monastery's carefully restored frescoes

↑ The peaceful inner courtyard lined by the arched passages of the monastery's cloisters

↑ A visitor taking photos inside the Casa Vicens, designed by Gaudí

EXPERIENCE MORE

CosmoCaixa

🏠 Carrer d'Isaac Newton 26
🚇 Avinguda del Tibidabo
🚌 17, 22, 58, 60, 73, 75, 196
🕐 10am–8pm daily 🚫 1 & 6
Jan, 25 Dec 🌐 cosmo
caixa.es

Revamped in 2004, the city's science museum is even more stimulating and interactive than its popular predecessor, which was housed in the Modernista building that still stands on site. Inside the glass-and-steel building, the museum has nine storeys, six of which are set underground, with exhibits covering the history of science, from the Big Bang to the computer age.

One of its most important pieces is a glasshouse containing a flooded forest,

re-creating the environs of the Amazon. The exhibit sprawls across 1,000 sq m (10,800 sq ft) and is inhabited by fish, amphibians, insects, reptiles, birds, mammals and plant species. Elsewhere, an interactive tour through Earth's geological history explains processes such as erosion and sedimentation. Its highlight is a fascinating Geological Wall that examines various types of rock, each originated from a different geological process.

Other exhibits include the Matter Room, which takes a look at the Big Bang theory; "Tecnorevolució", an interactive exploration of cutting-edge technological and scientific developments, such as nano-technology and robot eyes; and a 3D planetarium. There are also a number of

innovative temporary exhibitions on environmental issues, and family activities.

Casa Vicens

🏠 Carrer de les Carolines 20
🚇 Fontana, Lesseps 🕐 Apr–14 Oct: 10am–8pm daily;
15 Oct–Mar: 10am–3pm
Mon, 10am–7pm Tue–Sun
🚫 1 & 6 Jan, 25 Dec
🌐 casavicens.org

Built in the 1880s as a summer home for the Vicens family, this magnificent building was Antoni Gaudí's first major commission and is one of the earliest buildings to be designed in the Modernista style. The captivating façade of the Casa Vicens is an explosion of colour, at once austere and flamboyant, with Neo-Mudéjar elements that hark back to Spain's Moorish architecture. The building was declared a UNESCO World Heritage Site in 2005. Inside, sgraffito floral motifs point to

> The captivating façade of the Casa Vicens is an explosion of colour, at once austere and flamboyant, with Neo-Mudéjar elements that hark back to Spain's Moorish architecture.

an obsession with nature that would become one of Gaudí's signatures. Across the ground and first floors are perfectly preserved residential rooms, which feature original furniture designed by Gaudí and paintings by Catalan artist Francesc Torrescassana. The second floor is home to the permanent exhibition, which details the history of the house.

In typical Gaudí style, there is something of interest from top to bottom. Amble around the rooftop walkway which looks out at calming views of the Gràcia neighbourhood. Meanwhile down in the old coal cellar you'll find an underground bookshop.

Outside, the garden is the result of a 1925 extension and today home to

the pleasant Hofmann Café. After following one of the recommended walking routes passed out at the ticket desk, this charming spot is an ideal place to mull it all over with a cup of coffee and a pastry. Every Monday tickets to the house are offered at a reduced rate.

6
Parc de Joan Miró

Carrer d'Aragó 2
Tarragona ◷10am–dusk daily

Barcelona's 19th-century *escorxador* (slaughterhouse) was transformed into this unusual park in the 1980s – hence its alternative name, Parc de l'Escorxador.

The park is constructed on two planes: the lower plane, fringed with shady paths and studded with palm trees, is popular with dog walkers and for football kick-abouts; the upper is paved and dominated by the park's main attraction, a magnificent 1983 sculpture by the Catalan artist Joan Miró entitled *Dona i Ocell* (Woman and Bird). Standing 22 m (72 ft) high in the middle of a

pool, its surface is covered with colourful glazed tiles. The park is very popular with locals, making it a good place to get a taste of what Barcelona's like away from the main tourist hubs. Other attractions include a water feature, sports courts and several play areas for children.

←

Dona i Ocell, the statue by Miró himself that overlooks the Parc de Joan Miró

Visitors taking in the rainforest exhibit at CosmoCaixa

7

Tibidabo

🏠 Plaça del Tibidabo 3-4 🚌 Avda Tibidabo, then bus 196 & Funicular del Tibidabo; Peu del Funicular, then bus 111 & funicular de Vallvidrera 🚃 T2A from Plaça de Catalunya 🌐 tibidabo.cat

The name of this high vantage point is inspired by Tibidabo's views of the city and comes from the Latin *tibi dabo* (meaning "I shall give you") – a reference to the Temptation of Christ, when Satan took him up a mountain and offered him the world spread at his feet. One of the greatest draws to the area is the hugely popular **Parc d'Atraccions** (Amusement Park), which first opened in 1908. The rides were renovated in the 1980s. While the old ones retain their charm, the newer ones have the latest innovations. Standing at 517 m (1,696 ft), their location adds to the thrill. The amusement park offers a regular programme of events throughout the year, including parades and interactive shows for children. Also in the park is the Museu d'Autòmats, displaying automated toys, juke boxes and slot machines.

Tibidabo is crowned by the **Temple Expiatori del Sagrat Cor** (Church of the Sacred Heart). More often referred to as simply the "Temple of Tibidabo", this was built with religious zeal but little taste by Enric Sagnier between 1902 and 1911. Inside the church is split across two floors, with the interiors a mix of Roman and Gothic style. A lift (for which there is a small fee) takes you up to the feet of an enormous figure of Christ, where you'll find an even better vantage point for exceptional views across the city.

The heights of Tibidabo can be reached by Barcelona's last surviving tram. Just a short bus ride away is another viewpoint – the impressive Torre de Collserola.

Parc d'Atraccions
♿ 🏠 Plaça del Tibidabo 3 🕐 Hours vary, check website 🌐 tibidabo.cat

Temple Expiatori del Sagrat Cor
🏠 Cumbre del Tibidabo 📞 934 17 56 86 🕐 11am-8:45pm daily

→ Visitors looking out across the city from the Torre de Collserola's viewing platform

8

Torre Bellesguard

🏠 Carrer de Bellesguard 20
🚇 Avda Tibidabo 🚌 60, 123, 196, 🕐 10am–3pm Tue–Sun
🚫 1 & 6 Jan, 25 & 26 Dec
🌐 bellesguardgaudi.com

Bellesguard means "beautiful spot" and this place in the Collserola hills was chosen by the medieval Catalan kings as their summer home. The castle, built in 1408, was a favourite residence of Barcelona's Martí the Humanist.

The surrounding district of Sant Gervasi was developed in the 19th century, after the coming of the railway. In 1900, Gaudí built the present house

on the site of the castle, which had fallen badly into ruin. Its castellated look and the elongated, Gothic-inspired windows refer clearly to the original castle. The roof is topped by a distinctive Gaudí tower. Ceramic fish mosaics located by the main door symbolize Catalonia's past maritime power.

9

Torre de Collserola

🏠 Carretera de Vallvidrera al Tibidabo 🚇 Peu del Funicular, then bus 111 & Funicular de Vallvidrera
🕐 1–2pm Sat & Sun 🚫 1 & 6 Jan, 25, 26 & 31 Dec
🌐 torredecollserola.com

In this city that enjoys thrills, the ultimate ride is offered by the communications tower near Tibidabo mountain. A glass-sided lift swiftly reaches the top of this 288-m (944-ft) structure, standing atop a steep hill. Needle-like in form, it is a tubular steel mast on a concrete pillar, anchored by 12 huge steel cables. There are 13 levels; the top one has an observatory with a telescope and a public-viewing platform with a 360° view of the city, the sea and the mountain chain up on which Tibidabo sits.

Did You Know?

The Torre de Collserola was designed by English architect Norman Foster for the 1992 Olympics.

← The multicoloured neon lights of rides in Tibidabo's popular Parc d'Atraccions

↑ The well-maintained labyrinth at the Parc del Laberint d'Horta

10

Parc del Laberint d'Horta

⬜ Carrer Germans Desvalls, Passeig dels Castanyers ⬜ Mundet ⬜ Mar & Oct: 10am–7pm daily; Apr: 10am–8pm daily; May–Sep: 10am–9pm daily; Nov–Feb: 10am–6pm daily ⬜ lameva. barcelona.cat/en/enjoy-it/ parks-and-gardens

As you might suspect, given its name, the centrepiece of the city's oldest park, created in the 18th century for Joan Antoni Desvalls, Marquès de Llupià i d'Alfarràs, is a cypress maze.

Sloping steeply uphill, the semi-wild garden extends from the entrance beside the marquis's palace, home to a gardening school. It is a veritable compendium of aristocratic Baroque fantasies. Classical temples dedicated to Ariadne (who helped Theseus escape from the Minotaur's labyrinth) and Danae (mother of Perseus) flank the base of a monumental flight of steps that lead up to a Neo-Classical temple.

Elsewhere, there is a faux cemetery, an interpretation of a "romantic" garden and, in the woodland into which the garden eventually leads, a hermit's cave.

11

Museu del Disseny

⬜ Plaça de les Glòries Catalanes 37–38 ⬜ Glòries ⬜ 7, 92, 192, H12 ⬜ 10am–8pm Tue–Sun ⬜ 1 Jan, 1 May, 25 Dec ⬜ dhub-bcn.cat

With more than 70,000 objects, the Museu del Disseny (Design Museum) is a merging of the Decorative Arts, Ceramics, Textile and Clothing Museum, and the Graphic Arts Cabinet, which were previously housed at different sites across the city. The glass-and-zinc-clad building is a design statement in its own right, and was created by architects Josep Martorell, Oriol Bohigas and David Mackay.

The combined collection pieces together a long design history. Organized on broad thematic lines, it traces the evolution of the objects that surround us in our everyday lives, from the decorative arts

INSIDER TIP
Culture on the Cheap

To honour International Museum Day, each 18 May many of the city's museums throw open their doors for free – for many, it's the only day of the year that the fee is waived for visitors.

of past centuries (some artifacts date back to the Middle Ages) to contemporary design. The fascinating exhibits include furniture, clothing, jewellery, prints and posters, ceramics, glasswork and even exquisitely printed wallpaper. A varied programme of lectures and activities for children are held here, including textile and design workshops (ideal for young fashionistas). Tickets are valid for two days, so you have plenty of time to take in the

→

The modern, angular exterior of the Museu del Disseny at dusk

↑ Catalan artworks on display within the Museu Can Framis

Llibreria Altaïr

With two floors lined with travel books, comfy armchairs in quiet corners and a cute café, this spot is perfect for whiling away hours.

🏠 Gran Via de les Corts Catalanes 616
🌐 altair.es

Els Encants

This vast flea market in Poblenou has a rippling mirror roof that reflects the piles of clothes, furniture and bric-a-brac inside.

🏠 Avinguida Meridiana 69 🌐 encantsbcn.com

Palo Alto Market

Come to satisfy all your vintage, one-of-a-kind and epic-street-food needs. Live music and a party atmosphere make it an occasion.

🏠 Carrer dels Pellaires 30
🌐 palomarketfest.com

entire collection. Entry is free on Sunday afternoons.

Museu Can Framis

🏠 Carrer de Roc Boronat 116-126, Poblenou
Ⓜ Glòries, Poblenou 🚌 6, 7, 40, 42, 56, 141, 192, B25
🕐 11am-6pm Tue-Sat, 11am-2pm Sun 🔒 29 Jul-15 Sep, 25-26 & 31 Dec
🌐 fundaciovilacasas.com

The Can Framis museum occupies a renovated 18th-century wool factory, which is a monument to local industry. A modern building has been attached to the factory and its striking geometric architecture is worth seeing in itself. It is managed by the Vila Casa Foundation and holds a permanent exhibition, "The Existential Labyrinth", of around 300 works from the 1960s onwards. These works are by a range of artists born or living in Catalonia, like Tàpies, Llimós and Cuixart. The Espai A0 gallery hosts temporary exhibitions by local artists and photographers. The museum is surrounded by a park, which makes for a pleasant stroll.

TOP 4 BARCELONA BEACHES

Sant Miquel
Overlooked by Rebecca Horn's sculpture, this is an easy-to-access beach.
🚇 Barceloneta

Barceloneta
This strand is home to "Espai de Mar", which offers a whole host of fun activities (p92).
🚇 Barceloneta

Bogatell
One of the city's longest and busiest stretches of sand, it is particularly popular with families.
🚇 Llacuna

Mar Bella
This is Barcelona's unofficial gay beach, offering bars, DJs and cocktails.
🚇 Poblenou

13

El Poblenou

🏠 Rambla del Poblenou
🚇 Poblenou

El Poblenou is a trendy part of town where artists have built their studios in the defunct warehouses of the city's former industrial heartland. The area is centred on the Rambla del Poblenou, a quiet avenue that extends from Avinguda Diagonal down to the sea. Here, palm trees back a stretch of sandy beach. A walk around the quiet streets leading from the Rambla will reveal a few protected pieces of industrial architecture, legacies from the time when Barcelona was a thriving industrial hub.

Along the parallel Carrer del Ferrocarril is the Plaça de

Prim with low, whitewashed houses that are reminiscent of a small country town.

---

14 ♿

Museu de Ciències Naturals - Museu Blau

🏠 Plaça Leonardo da Vinci 4-5, Parc del Fòrum
🚇 Maresme-Fòrum 🚌 H16
🕙 10am-6pm Tue-Fri (to 7pm Mar-Sep), 1-7pm Sat, 10am-8pm Sun 🚫 Mon; 1 Jan, 1 May, 24 Jun, 25 Dec
🌐 museuciencies.cat

The Natural Science Museum is a Barcelona institution. More than 100 years old, it contains 3 million specimens

One of the exhibits at (inset) the Natural Science Museum ↓

in the fields of mineralogy, palaeontology, zoology and botany.

Previously located in the Old Town, it is now housed in the Parc del Fòrum in a modern, innovative building designed by architects Herzog & de Meuron, who also created the Planet Life exhibition. This vast exhibition sprawls across a third of the museum's space and is essentially a journey through the history of life and its evolution to the present day. The high-tech museum is split into three sections: "Biography of the Earth", "Earth Today" and "Islands of Science". State-of-the-art interactive and audiovisual displays take the visitor on a journey of discovery, with well-distilled explanations of the subject. There are also temporary exhibitions, a Media Library and a "Science Nest" for children up to age six at weekends, where images and sound effects re-create different natural surroundings.

⑮

Estació del Nord

🚇 **Avinguda de Vilanova**
🚇 **Arc de Triomf**

Only the 1861 façade and the grand 1915 entrance remain of this former railway station, now remodelled as a sports centre, a police headquarters, and the city's bus station.

Two elegant, blue-tiled sculptures, *Espiral arbrada (Branched Spiral)* and *Cel caigut (Fallen Sky)* by American sculptor Beverly Pepper (1992), sweep through the park opposite the station. At Avinguda de Vilanova 12 is a carefully restored Modernista building constructed as a power station in 1897 by architect Pere Falqués.

Nearby, on Carrer de Zamora, is the Teatre Nacional de Catalunya – a vast temple to culture by Barcelona architect Ricardo Bofill – and the state-of-the-art concert hall L'Auditori.

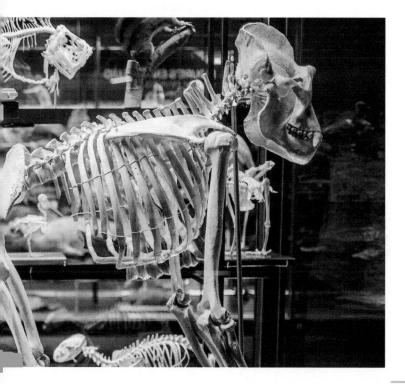

A LONG WALK
POBLENOU

Distance 3.5 km (2 miles) **Nearest metro**
Glòries **Time** 1 hour

The trendy district of Poblenou once had the highest concentration of smoke-belching factories in Catalonia. By the 1960s, these had gone out of business or moved to the outskirts, leaving their old buildings to decay. With the 1992 Olympics came an impetus for recovery and since then, Poblenou's warehouses have been spruced up and converted into chic studios for artists. New developments brought clubs and restaurants, in a heady mix of industrial archaeology and contemporary culture.

Plaça de les Glòries Catalanes *is an area of ongoing redevelopment.*

A major thoroughfare, **Avinguda Diagonal** *has a wide seaward extension.*

PLAÇA DE LES GLÒRIES CATALANES
START
Glòries Ⓜ
Museu del Disseny
Torre Agbar
🚉 Ca l'Aranyó
AVINGUDA DIAGONAL
CARRER DE BOLIVIA
CARRER DE TÀNGER
POBLENOU

It's worth visiting the **Museu del Disseny** *(p156) even if it's just to admire the curious shape of this local landmark.*

The **Torre Agbar**, *a domed cylindrical tower of 33 floors, has been described as an upended blue cigar.*

The main street of Poblenou, quiet **Rambla del Poblenou** *(p158) leads down to the sea.*

Dr Josep Trueta

DEL

RAMBLA

CARRER DE LA LLACUNA

The **memorial to Dr Josep Trueta** *honours a Poblenou-born surgeon who saved lives during the Civil War.*

El Tio Chel
Casino l'Aliança de Poblenou

El Tio Che, *a shop founded in 1912, sells ice cream and turrón (a sweet made of almonds).*

CARRER

The **Casino de l'Alliança de Poblenou** *is a concert hall, not a gambling enterprise as its name might suggest.*

| 0 metres | 300 | N |
| 0 yards | 300 | |

↑ The glass-and-zinc building of the Museu del Disseny

BEYOND
THE CENTRE

Poblenou

The public library at **Carrer del Joncar** 35 is housed in a building that used to be a textile factory.

↑ Wandering along the Rambla del Poblenou

On the corner of Carrer de Ramon Turró and Espronceda is a **garden** dedicated to Mahatma Gandhi, with a sculpture of him by Adolfo Pérez Esquivel.

On the corner with **Carrer de Provençals** rises a graceful flat-topped chimney, the highest in Barcelona.

Pere IV

Fluvià

Selva de Mar

Selva de Mar

FINISH

M Poblenou

Biblioteca Poblenou

Jardins de Gandhi

Chimney

Parc de Diagonal Mar

Mercat de la Unió

Torre de les Aigües

TAULAT

PLAÇA DEL PRIM

PASSEIG DEL TAULAT

PASSEIG DEL TAULAT

PASSEIG DE GARCIA FÀRIA

The **Mercat de la Unió** is the district's market, where locals stock up on fresh produce.

At **Plaça del Prim** you'll see gnarled, leaning ombu trees and low whitewashed houses.

The round, red-brick **Torre de les Aigües** was built to raise and store water from the nearby Besos river.

A LONG WALK
GRÀCIA

BEYOND THE CENTRE
Gràcia

Distance 2.5 km (1.5 miles) **Nearest metro**
Plaça Joan Carles I **Time** 45 minutes

When you cross the Avinguda Diagonal and plunge into the maze of streets and small squares, it is easy to think that you have left the city behind and entered a village. Since Gràcia became part of Barcelona in 1897, it has never lost its sense of identity. During the day, it feels calmly removed from the pace of modern metropolitan life. In summer and in the evening, however, crowds are drawn to its shops and nightlife.

Locator Map
For more detail see p143

There is a civil war air-raid shelter at Plaça Diamant – open at weekends by appointment (call 93 219 61 34).

*Inspired by Moorish architecture, **Casa Vicens** (p150) is Gaudí's early work.*

Plaça de Trilla *was inaugurated under the name of Queen Amàlia.*

Plaça Virreina *with the church of Sant Joan is one of Gràcia's most agreeable squares.*

Plaça del Sol *is a nightlife hub popularly known as Plaça dels Encants.*

*On Gran de Gràcia, you can see the handsome stained-glass bay windows above **La Colmena patisseria**.*

*The **Casa Bonaventura Ferrer** has stonework of swirling leaves.*

Plaça Revolució de Setembre de 1868 *commemorates the coup d'état led by General Prim.*

*On **Plaça de la Vila de Gràcia**, a 33-m (108-ft) clock tower is overlooked by the sky-blue façade of local government headquarters.*

START/FINISH

*From **Plaça Joan Carles I**, the Passeig de Gràcia continues briefly as a modest avenue.*

*The **Casa Fuster** has been converted into a hotel.*

0 metres 200
0 yards 200

N

↑ The brightly decorated
Casa Vicens, designed
by Antoni Gaudí

CATALONIA

It was at Empúries, on Catalonia's Costa Brava ("wild coast"), that the Romans first set foot on the land that they would name Hispania. After the fall of the Roman Empire and a period of Visigothic, then Moorish rule, it was conquered by the Franks in the early 9th century. It later enjoyed independence as the County of Barcelona before being incorporated into the Crown of Aragón as the autonomous Principality of Catalonia. This regional autonomy survived the union of Castile and Aragón in 1492, persisting until 1714, when Felipe V centralized the Spanish government in Castile.

In the second half of the 19th century, the independence movement reemerged, but any progress towards the reestablishment of Catalan autonomy came to a brutal stop when Franco came to power in the 1930s.

Following Franco's death, full autonomy was restored to Catalonia and its Generalitat in 1979. Since then, the independence movement has gathered significant momentum, reaching a head in 2017 when a referendum saw Catalonians vote to become an independent republic. This referendum was declared illegal by the Spanish government, and was boycotted by unionist factions, however the Catalan push for independence continues.

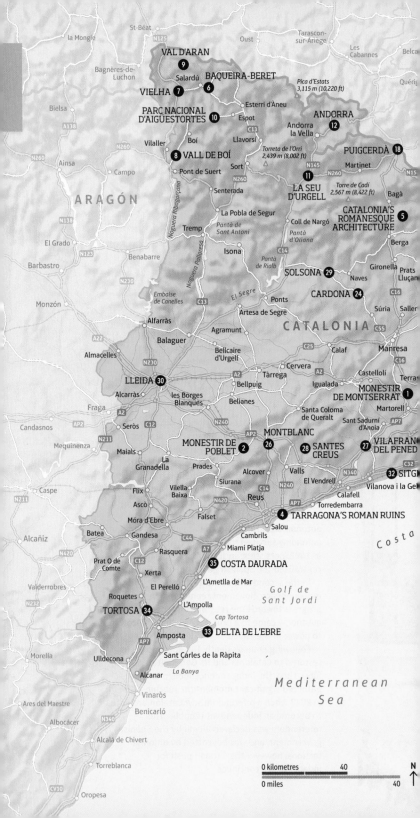

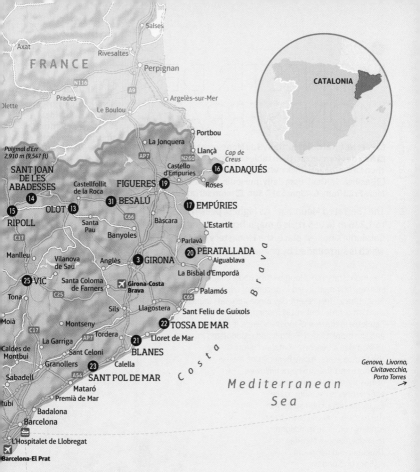

CATALONIA

Must Sees

1 Monestir de Montserrat
2 Monestir de Poblet
3 Girona
4 Tarragona's Roman Ruins
5 Catalonia's Romanesque
    Architecture

Experience More

6 Baqueira-Beret
7 Vielha
8 Vall de Boí
9 Val d'Aran
10 Parc Nacional d'Aigüestortes
11 La Seu d'Urgell
12 Andorra
13 Olot
14 Sant Joan de les Abadesses
15 Ripoll
16 Cadaqués

17 Empúries
18 Puigcerdà
19 Figueres
20 Peratallada
21 Blanes
22 Tossa de Mar
23 Sant Pol de Mar
24 Cardona
25 Vic
26 Montblanc
27 Vilafranca del Penedès
28 Santes Creus
29 Solsona
30 Lleida
31 Besalú
32 Sitges
33 Delta de L'Ebre
34 Tortosa
35 Costa Daurada

❶ 〈⚔️〉 〈Ⓜ️〉 〈🖥️〉

MONESTIR DE MONTSERRAT

🏛️ Parc Natural de la Muntanya de Montserrat, Barcelona
🚡 Aeri de Montserrat, then cable car; Monistrol-Enllaç, then La Cremallera rack railway 🚌 From Barcelona
🕐 Basilica: 7:30am-8pm daily; museum: 10am-5:45pm Mon-Fri, 10am-6:45pm Sat & Sun 🌐 montserratvisita.com

The "Serrated Mountain", its highest peak rising to 1,236 m (4,055 ft), is a magnificent setting for Catalonia's holiest place, the Monastery of Montserrat, which is surrounded by chapels and hermits' caves.

The monastery has a long history, and a chapel on the site was first mentioned in documents dating from the 9th century. The present-day monastery was founded in the 11th century but in 1811, when the French attacked Catalonia in the War of Independence, it was destroyed and the monks killed. Rebuilt and repopulated in 1844, it was a beacon of Catalan culture during the Franco years. Today Benedictine monks live here and the site has a hallowed atmosphere. One of the most magical experiences is listening to the Escolania boys' choir singing in the basilica. You can catch their echoing voices at 1pm Monday to Friday, 6:45pm Monday to Thursday and noon and 6:45pm on Sundays.

△ GREAT VIEW
Natural Wonder

Many locations in the Parc Natural de la Muntanya de Montserrat offer great views of Montserrat's tooth-shaped rock formations. Bird-watchers will want their binoculars at the ready as birds of prey soar above.

Gothic cloister

The museum has a collection of 19th- and 20th-century Catalan paintings. It also displays liturgical items from the Holy Land.

Plaça de Santa Maria's focal points are two wings of the Gothic cloister built in 1476. The modern monastery was designed by Françesc Folguera.

Inner courtyard

↑ Monestir de Montserrat, in its dramatic setting below the mountain

The mountain towering behind the Monestir de Montserrat ↑

Agapit Vallmitjana sculpted Christ and the apostles on the basilica's Neo-Renaissance façade in 1900.

The Black Virgin (La Moreneta) looks down from behind the altar. Protected behind glass, her wooden orb protrudes for pilgrims to touch.

The domed basilica interior

↑ The awe-inspiring interior of the domed basilica

The rack railway (La Cremallera), follows a rail line built in 1880.

Cable car to Aeri de Montserrat station

THE VIRGIN OF MONTSERRAT

The small wooden statue of La Moreneta (literally "the dark one") is said to have been made by St Luke and brought here by St Peter in AD 50. Centuries later, the statue is believed to have been hidden from the Moors in the nearby Santa Cova (Holy Cave). Carbon dating suggests, however, that the statue was carved around the 12th century. In 1881 La Maroneta became patroness of Catalonia.

The Monestir de Poblet, surrounded by golden vines ↑

② ⊘ Ⓜ ▣

MONESTIR DE POBLET

⌂ Off N240, 10 km (6 miles) from Montblanc, Tarragona ▣ L'Espluga de Francolí, then taxi ▣ Tarragona ◷ Mid-Mar-mid-Oct: 10am-12:30pm & 3-5:50pm daily; mid-Oct-mid-Mar: 10am-12:30pm & 3-5:25pm daily ◷ 1 Jan, 6 Jul, 25 & 26 Dec ◧ poblet.cat

The largest monastery in the "Cistercian triangle", the Monastery of Santa Maria de Poblet is a haven of tranquillity and a resting place of kings. At sunset, it almost seems to glow in heavenly light.

The Monestir de Poblet was the first and most important of three Cistercian monasteries that helped to consolidate power in Catalonia after it had been recaptured from the Moors by Ramon Berenguer IV. Despite this former importance, Poblet was abandoned and fell into disrepair as a result of the Ecclesiastical confiscations of 1835. Restoration began in 1930 and monks returned in 1940.

> ### THE CISTERCIAN TRIANGLE
> Built in the 12th century, the monasteries of Poblet, Vallbona de les Monges and Santes Creus are captivating examples of Gothic architecture, and each has served as the final resting place of Catalan royalty at one point or another. A 100-km (60-mile) drive will take you around all three. No longer used by a religious order, Santes Creus offers visitors the best opportunity to explore a Cistercian monastery.

Wine cellar

The 12th-century refectory is a vaulted hall with an octagonal fountain and a pulpit.

Royal doorway

Museum

1156
Monastery at Vallbona de les Monges founded

1336–87
Reign of Pere the Ceremonious, who designates Poblet a royal pantheon

1835
Disentailment of monasteries; Poblet ravaged royal pantheon

1952
▽ Tombs reconstructed; royal remains returned

Timeline

1150
Santes Creus and Poblet monasteries are founded

1196
△ Alfonso II is the first king to be buried here

1479
Juan II, last king of Aragón, buried here

1940
Monks return

The vast 87-m (285-ft) dormitory dates from the 13th century.

The Gothic scriptorium was converted into a library in the 17th century.

Former kitchen

The perfectly square chapterhouse has tiers of benches for the monks.

Sant Esteve cloister

↑ The cloisters, with capitals carved with scrollwork

Parlour cloister

Behind the stone altar, supported by Romanesque columns, an alabaster reredos fills the apse.

New sacristy

The tombs in the pantheon of kings were begun in 1359. In 1950 the sculptures were restored by Frederic Marès.

The evocative, vaulted cloisters were built in the 12th and 13th centuries and were the centre of monastic life.

The Abbey Church, large and unadorned, with three naves, is a typical Cistercian building.

Baroque church façade

← The many rooms that make up the Monestir de Poblet

❸

GIRONA

🏛 Girona ✈🚌🚆 ℹ Rambla de la Llibertat 1;
🌐 www.girona.cat/turisme

This handsome town puts on its best face beside the Riu Onyar, where colourful buildings rise above the water. These were built in the 19th century to replace sections of the city wall damaged during an 1809 siege by French troops. Most of the rest of the ramparts are intact and make up the Passeig Arqueològic (Archaeological Walk), which runs around the city. Behind the houses, the Rambla de la Llibertat is lined with shops and cafés.

The museum's most famous item is a large, well-preserved 11th- to 12th-century tapestry, called *The Creation*. There are also Romanesque paintings.

---

①

Museu d'Història dels Jueus

🏛 Carrer de la Força 8 📞 972 21 67 61 🕐 Jul & Aug: 10am-8pm Mon-Sat, 10am-2pm Sun; Sep-Jun: 10am-2pm Mon & Sun, 10am-6pm Tue-Sat 🗓 1 & 6 Jan, 25 & 26 Dec

Amid the maze of alleyways in the old town is the former Jewish quarter of El Call. One of the West's most important Jewish areas during medieval times, it is now home to the Museu d'Història dels Jueus, which gives a history of Girona's Jews, who were expelled in the late 15th century.

②

Cathedral

🏛 Plaça de la Catedral 🕐 Apr-Jun, Sep & Oct: 10am-6:30pm daily; Jul & Aug: 10am-7:30pm daily; Nov-Mar: 10am-5:30pm daily 🌐 catedraldegirona.cat

The style of Girona Cathedral's solid west face is pure Catalan Baroque; the cloister and tower, Romanesque; but the rest of the building is Gothic. The single nave is the widest in the world. Behind the altar is a marble throne called "Charlemagne's Chair" after the Frankish king whose troops took Girona in AD 785.

③

Museu d'Art

🏛 Pujada de la Catedral 12 🕐 May-Sep: 10am-7pm Tue-Sat, 10am-2pm Sun; Oct-Apr: 10am-6pm Tue-Sat, 10am-2pm Sun 🗓 1 & 6 Jan, 24-26 & 31 Dec 🌐 museuart.com

This former episcopal palace is one of Catalonia's best art galleries, with works ranging from the Romanesque period to the 20th century, including ecclesiastical items. Highlights are 10th-century carvings, a silver-clad altar from Sant Pere de Rodes and a 12th-century beam from Cruïlles.

← Colourful apartment buildings lining the Riu Onyar in Girona

Museu d'Història de Girona

📍 Carrer de la Força 27
📞 972 22 22 29 🕐 May-Sep:
10:30am-6:30pm Tue-Sat,
10:30am-1:30pm Sun; Oct-
Apr: 10:30am-5:30pm Tue-
Sat, 10:30am-1:30pm Sun

This museum is housed in a former convent and you can still explore the cemetery.

Monestir de Sant Pere de Galligants

📍 Carrer de Santa Llúcia 8
📞 972 20 26 32 🕐 Jun-
Sep: 10am-7pm Tue-Sat,
10am-2pm Sun; Oct-
May: 10am-6pm Tue-Sat,
10am-2pm Sun

This Romanesque temple is worth a visit for its stone

capitals, depicting a variety of motifs, including scenes from the New Testament, mythical beasts and geometric patterns.

Basílica de Sant Feliu

📍 Pujada de Sant Feliu 29
📞 972 42 71 89 🕐 10am-
5:30pm Mon-Sat,
1-5:30pm Sun

Begun in the 14th century, this staunch basilica was built over the tombs of St Felix and St Narcissus.

Museu del Cinema

📍 Carrer de la Sèquia 1
🕐 Hours vary, check website
🌐 museudelcinema.cat

A film buff's paradise, the Museu del Cinema offers a wide selection of exhibitions. The Tomàs Mallol Collection is particularly impressive, with around 20,000 objects that tell the history of the still image as well as motion pictures.

Must See

EAT

El Celler de Can Roca
This three-Michelin-starred restaurant serves traditional dishes with a twist.

📍 Carrer de Can Sunyer 48 🕐 Sun-Mon, Tue lunch 🌐 celler canroca.com

€€€

Banys Àrabs

📍 Carrer del Rei Ferran el Catòlic s/n 🕐 Hours vary, check website 🕐 1 & 6 Jan, 25 & 26 Dec 🌐 banys arabs.org

Despite their name, the Banys Àrabs were built under King Alfons I in the late 12th century, about 300 years after the Moors had left. The most striking feature is the octagonal pool, with a domed ceiling.

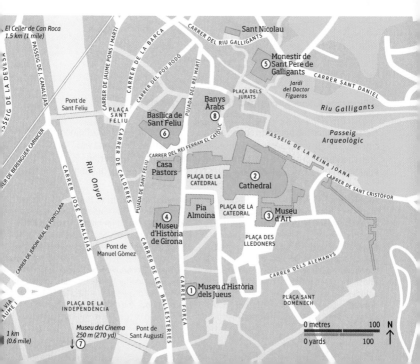

4 🚲 🚠

TARRAGONA'S ROMAN RUINS

🏠 Tarragona ✈ Reus Airport 🚉 🚌 ℹ Carrer de los Caballeros 14; www.mnat.cat

Today an industrial port, Tarragona stands on the site of the oldest Roman city in Spain. The archaeological ensemble of Tarraco, as Tarragona was then called, comprises the most important Roman ruins in the Iberian Peninsula. The site was declared a UNESCO World Heritage Site in 2000.

The Romans established Tarraco as a base from which to conquer Iberia, fortifying the imperial town with thick walls and sentry towers. The town's great amphitheatre, forums and circus, as well as numerous temples, can be visited today on the Roman Route designed by the Museu Nacional Arqueològic de Tarragona, whose important collection of Roman artifacts includes bronze tools and beautiful mosaics.

A walk along the remains of the old Roman walls that line Passeig Arqueològic takes you past the Casa Canals, an 18th-century stately home built into the Roman wall. Around the corner the Fòrum Provincial now bustles with bars and restaurants. Stone steps takes you up to the *recinte de culte*, an ancient site of worship.

Atop the cliffs, at the end of Rambla Nova, is the magnificent Amfiteatre Romà – and great sea views. Nearby, the Praetorium, a Roman tower, now displays excavated artifacts in rooms above the cavernous passageways of the Roman circus, where you can take a tour.

The soaring arches of the Aqüeducte de les Ferreres pass over the hiking trails of wooded "Devil Ravine".

Must See

EAT

A3Mans

Sample Catalan cuisine with a global inflection at this atmospheric cellar-restaurant with an excellent wine list.

⌂ Carrer d'en Salinas 5
☎ 977 91 57 43

€€€

DRINK

El Vergel

Homemade vermouth and organic wines round off creative plant-based fare at this uber-hip spot near the corner of the Roman Circus. Try the vegan chorizo.

⌂ Carrer Major 13 🌐 el vergeltarragona.com

€€€

① The carved marble sarcophagus of Hippolytus at the Praetorium dates to the 2nd century AD.

② Tourists explore the subterranean gallery of the ancient Roman Circus.

③ The well-preserved Amfiteatre Romà backed by turquoise seas

GREAT VIEW
Aqüeducte de les Ferreres

Walk along the central ridge of this magnificent 2nd-century aquaduct that once linked ancient Tarraco with the Riu Francolí for sublime 360° views of woodland and the city. It is in Parc Ecohistòric del Pont del Diable, 4 km (2 miles) from Tarragona centre.

CATALONIA'S ROMANESQUE ARCHITECTURE

🛈 Centre del Romànic de la Vall de Boí: Carrer del Batalló 5, Vall de Boi, www.centreromanic.com; Monastery of Sant Pere de Galligants, Carrer de Santa Llúcia 8, Girona, www.macgirona.cat

Strewn across northern Catalonia is an exceptional collection of medieval buildings constructed between the 11th and 13th centuries. Built in a distinctive local variant of the Romanesque style that swept Europe during that time, more than 2,000 examples of these buildings survive.

Most of Catalonia's surviving Romanesque buildings are churches, with lofty bell towers, barrel-vaulted naves, rounded arches and imaginative sculpture, and remarkable wall paintings. In the Girona Pyrenees, Sant Pere de Galligants, with its elaborate capitals and octagonal bell tower, is home to the Girona branch of Museu d'Arqueologia de Catalunya. In nearby Ripoll several Benedictine monasteries survive, including the Santa Maria de Ripoll with its more typical five-storey bell tower and famous portal.

Westwards, in the Vall de Boí *(p178)*, nine sights from the 11th and 12th centuries comprise the Romanesque ensemble, a World Heritage Site. The Centre del Romànic, in Boí, has maps of the Romanesque route, which takes in Sant Climent in Taüll and Sant Joan in the village of Boí itself, although their original frescoes are currently displayed at the Museu Nacional d'Art de Catalunya *(p130)* in Barcelona.

PORTAL OF MONESTIR DE SANTA MARIA DE RIPOLL

The portal of the church of the former Benedictine monastery at Ripoll is known as "The Ripoll Bible" for its well-preserved allegorical carvings. Although the church was founded in 879 and rebuilt under Abbot Oliva in 1032, the portal was added only in the late 12th century. In this fine piece of Romanesque decoration, Christ sits above the doorway amid beasts, which symbolize the Apostles. There are seven biblical friezes running the length of the wall, including the stories of Moses and Solomon. The topmost frieze over the tympanum represents the old men of the Apocalypse.

① The square bell tower of Sant Climent soars over Taüll in Vall de Boí.

② The Baldachin of Ribes from San Clemente de Taüll can be seen at the Museu Episcopal de Vic.

③ Visitors congregate under the barrel-vaulted nave of Sant Pere de Besalú.

Did You Know?

Sant Pere de Galligants has housed an archaeological museum since 1857.

↑ Sant Pere de Galligants atmospherically lit as dusk settles over Girona

EXPERIENCE MORE

6

Baqueira-Beret

🏠 Lleida 🚌 🌐 baqueira.es

This extensive ski resort, one of the best in all of Spain, is popular with both the public and the Spanish royal family. In the winter months, there is reliable snow cover across over 100 runs at altitudes from 1,520 m to 2,470 m (4,990 ft to 8,100 ft). The resort has some good beginners' slopes, although intermediate and advanced skiers will benefit most from the pistes on offer.

Popular with the Romans for their fantastic thermal springs, Baqueira and Beret were once separate mountain villages. The villages merged to form a single resort once they became popular destinations for skiing and other winter sports. These days the thermal springs are appreciated by tired skiers.

↓ Skiers pausing at the top of a wide piste in Baqueira-Beret

---

Did You Know?

Catalonia has three official languages: Catalan, Spanish and Aranès.

7

Vielha

🏠 Lleida 🚌 🛈 Carrer Sarriulèra 10; 973 64 01 10

A convenient base for skiing at Baqueira-Beret, the capital of the Val d'Aran retains its medieval past. The Romanesque church of Sant Miquel has a 12th-century crucifix, the *Mig Aran Christ*. It formed part of a larger carving representing the Descent from the Cross. The **Musèu dera Val d'Aran** is devoted to Aranese culture.

Musèu dera Val d'Aran

🌐 🏠 Carrer Major 26 📞 973 64 18 15 🕐 10am–1pm & 5–8pm Mon–Sat, 10am–1pm Sun 🚫 Pub hols, Mon mid-Sep–mid-Jun

---

8

Vall de Boí

🏠 Lleida N230 🚗 La Pobla de Segur 🚌 Pont de Suert 🛈 Barruera; www.vallboi.com

This small valley located on the edge of the Parc Nacional d'Aigüestortes is dotted with tiny villages, many of which are built around magnificent Catalan Romanesque churches (p176).

Dating from the 11th and 12th centuries, these churches are distinguished by their tall belfries, such as the six-storey bell tower of the Església de Santa Eulàlia at Erill la Vall. The two churches at Taüll, Sant Climent and Santa Maria, have superb frescoes.

Between 1919 and 1923, the originals were taken for safekeeping to the Museu Nacional d'Art de Catalunya (p130) in Barcelona, where their settings have been recreated. Replicas now stand in their place. You can climb the towers of Sant Climent for superb views of the surrounding countryside.

Autumnal colours tumbling down the slopes of the Val d'Aran

Other churches in the area worth visiting include those at Coll, for its fine ironwork; Barruera; and Durro, which has another massive bell tower.

At the head of the valley is the hamlet of Caldes de Boí, popular for its bubbling thermal springs and nearby ski facilities. It also makes a good base for exploring the Parc Nacional d'Aigüestortes (p180), the entrance to which is only 5 km (3 miles) from here.

⑨
Val d'Aran

🅰Lleida 🚍Vielha 🚇Carrer Sarriulèra 10, Vielha; 973 64 01 10

This valley of valleys – aran means valley – is a lovely 600-sq-km (230-sq-mile) haven of forests and meadows filled with flowers, surrounded by towering mountain peaks. It was formed by the Riu Garona, which rises in the area and flows out to France as the Garonne. With no proper link to the outside world until 1924, when a road was built over the Bonaigua Pass, the valley was cut off from the rest of Spain for most of the winter. Snow still blocks the narrow pass from November to April, but today access is easy through the Túnel de Vielha from El Pont de Suert.

Because it faces north, the Val d'Aran has a climate similar to that of the Atlantic coast. Many rare wild flowers and butterflies flourish in the conditions created by the shady slopes and damp breezes. The valley is also a famous habitat for many species of narcissus.

Tiny villages have grown up beside the Riu Garona, often around Romanesque churches, notably at Bossòst, Salardú, Escunhau and Arties. The valley is also ideal for outdoor sports such as skiing and walking. This area even has its own language, Aranès (Aranese in English).

BUTTERFLIES OF THE VAL D'ARAN

A huge variety of butterflies is found in the mountains and valleys of the Pyrenees. The isolated Val d'Aran is home to as many as 91 species, including rare subspecies such as the marbled white (*Melanargia galathea*) and the map butterfly (*Araschnia levana*). Lepidopterists hiking through the meadows between May and July may see black-spotted shepherd's fritillary (*Boloria pales*), boldly striped Spanish festoons (*Zerynthia rumina*), delicate clouded Apollos (*Parnassius mnemosyne*), grizzled skipper (*Pyrgus malvae*) and chequered skipper (*Carterocephalus palaemon*) fluttering between open-faced daisies and the coiling labellum of the lizard orchid.

CHEQUERED SKIPPER

CLOUDED APOLLO

GRIZZLED SKIPPER

A lone hiker passing glassy lakes in the Parc Nacional d'Aigüestortes

⑩

Parc Nacional d'Aigüestortes

⌂ Lleida 🚌🚗 Ⓦ parcs naturals.gencat.cat/en/ aiguestortes

The pristine mountain scenery of Catalonia's only national park is among the most spectacular that can be found in the Pyrenees.

Established in 1955, the park's full title is Parc Nacional d'Aigüestortes i Estany de Sant Maurici, named after the *estany* (lake) of Sant Maurici in the east and the Aigüestortes

(literally, twisted waters) area in the west. The main village is the mountain settlement of Espot, although you can access the park from Boí in the west. Around the park are waterfalls and some 150 lakes and tarns which, in an earlier era, were scoured by glaciers to depths of up to 50 m (164 ft).

The finest scenery is around Sant Maurici lake, beneath the twin shards of the Serra dels Encantats (Mountains of the Enchanted). From here, there is a variety of walks, while to the south is the dramatic vista of Estany Negre, the highest and deepest tarn in the park.

Early summer on the lower valley slopes is marked by rhododendrons, while in later months wild lilies bloom in the forests of fir, beech and silver birch.

The park is also home to a variety of wildlife. Chamois (also known as izards) live on the mountain screes and in the meadows, while beavers and otters can be spotted by the lakes. Golden eagles nest on mountain ledges, and

grouse and capercaillie are found in the woods.

In summer, the park is popular with walkers, while in winter, the snow-covered mountains are perfect for a spot of cross-country skiing.

PICTURE PERFECT
Stunning Sant Maurici Lake

For postcard-perfect snaps, head to the lake's eastern shore. Here the turquoise waters provide a shimmering mirror for the fir-dotted hillsides rising up to join the mountains.

LES QUATRE BARRES

The four red bars on the *senyera*, the Catalan flag, represent the four provinces: Barcelona, Girona, Lleida and Tarragona. The design derives from a legend about Guifré el Pelós, Count of Barcelona, who received a call for help from Charles the Bald, King of the West Franks. Guifré turned the tide of battle, but was mortally wounded. Charles dipped his fingers in Guifré's blood and dragged them across his plain gold shield, giving him a grant of arms.

a 10th-century copy of St Beatus of Liébana's *Commentary on the Apocalypse*.

Museu Diocesà

⊗ ⌂ Plaça del Deganat
☎ 973 35 32 42 ⏰ Mid-Mar-May & Oct: 10am-1:30pm & 4-6pm daily; Jun-mid-Sep: 10am-1:30pm & 4-7pm daily; Nov-mid-Mar: 10am-1:30pm daily ⊘ 1 Jan, 25 Dec
🌐 museudiocesaurgell.org

---

⑫

Andorra

⌂ Principality of Andorra
🚌 Andorra la Vella ℹ Plaça de la Rotonda, Andorra la Vella; www.visit andorra.com

Andorra occupies 464 sq km (179 sq miles) of the Pyrenees between France and Spain. In 1993, it became fully independent and held its first ever democratic elections. Since 1278, it had been an autonomous feudal state under the jurisdiction of the Spanish bishop of La Seu d'Urgell and the French Count of Foix (a title adopted by the President of France). These are still the ceremonial joint heads of state.

Andorra's official language is Catalan, though French and Castilian are also spoken by most residents. For many years, Andorra has been a tax-free paradise for shoppers, a fact reflected in the crowded stores of the capital, Andorra la Vella. Nearby

⑪

La Seu d'Urgell

⌂ Lleida 🚌 ℹ Carrer Major 8; www.turismeseu.com

This Pyrenean town became a bishopric in the 6th century. Feuds between the bishops of Urgell and the Counts of Foix over land gave rise to Andorra in the 13th century. The cathedral has a Romanesque statue of Santa Maria d'Urgell. The **Museu Diocesà** contains

Les Escaldes, Sant Julià de Lòria and El Pas de la Casa (the towns nearest the Spanish and French borders), have also become busy shopping centres.

Most visitors never see Andorra's rural charms, which match those of other parts of the Pyrenees. The region is excellent for walkers. One of the main routes leads to the Cercle de Pessons, a bowl of lakes in the east. In the north is the picturesque Sorteny valley, with farmhouses converted into snug restaurants.

←

The simple stone cathedral in La Seu d'Urgell

The marina of Cadaqués on the Costa Brava, aglow at dusk

13

Olot

🏛 Girona 🚌 ℹ Carrer del Francesc Fàbregas 6; www.turismeolot.com

This sizeable market town sits at the centre of a dramatic landscape pockmarked with extinct volcanoes. But it was an earthquake in 1474 that destroyed its medieval past.

In the 18th century, the town's textile industry spawned the "Olot school" of art, where cotton fabrics were printed with drawings. In 1783, the Public School of Drawing was founded. Much of the school's work, including paintings such as Joaquim Vayreda's *Les Falgueres*, is in the surprisingly enriching **Museu Comarcal de la Garrotxa**. Modernista sculptor Miquel Blay's damsels support the balcony.

Museu Comarcal de la Garrotxa

🕸 🏛 Carrer Hospici 8
📞 972 27 11 66 🕙 10am-1pm & 3-6pm Tue-Fri, 11am-2pm & 4-7pm Sat, 11am-2pm Sun

The broad, pointed arch bridge stretching to Sant Joan de les Abadesses ↑

14 🄜

Sant Joan de les Abadesses

🏛 Girona 🚌 ℹ Plaça de l'Abadia 9; www.santjoan delesabadesses.cat

A fine, 12th-century Gothic bridge arches over the Riu Ter to this unassuming market town, whose main attraction is its monastery.

Founded in 885, the monastery was a gift from Guifré, the first count of Barcelona, to his daughter, the first abbess. The church has little decoration except for a wooden calvary, *The Descent from the Cross*. Though made in 1150, it looks modern. The figure of a thief on the left was burnt during the Civil War and has been replaced so skilfully that it is hard to tell it is new. The museum also features beautiful Baroque and Renaissance altarpieces.

←

The intricately carved sculpture at the door to Museu Comarcal de la Garrotxa in Olot

To the north are the small towns of Camprodon and Beget, both worth visiting for their handsome Romanesque churches. In Camprodon, seek out its renowned *botifarra* sausage in the delis around the central square, Plaça del Carme.

15

Ripoll

🏛 Girona 🚌🚆 ℹ Plaça Abat Oliba; www.ripoll.cat

Once a tiny mountain base from which raids against the Moors were made, Ripoll is now best known for the Monestir de Santa Maria *(p176)*, founded in 879. The town is called the "cradle of Catalonia" as the monastery was the power base of Guifré el Pelós (Wilfred the Hairy), founder of the House of Barcelona. He is buried here. In the later 12th century, the west portal was decorated with what are regarded as the finest Romanesque carvings in Spain. This and the cloister are the only parts of the

> **In the 18th century, the town's textile industry spawned the "Olot school" of art, where cotton fabrics were printed with drawings.**

original medieval monastery to have survived.

Ripoll has always been an industrious area, and the best place to explore its dynamic heritage is at the Museu Etnogràfic de Ripoll, which takes visitors through the region's history of agriculture, nail and weaponry making, the textile industry and more. The permanent collection is exhibited across three floors, and there are also temporary exbihits throughout the year.

Every July and August, the town hosts the Ripoll International Music Festival, which provides an enjoyable programme of classical music concerts.

↑ Passing below the Romanesque portal of the Monestir de Santa Maria in Ripoll

STAY

Hotel El Ciervo
This cosy hotel near the Baqueira-Beret ski resort is the perfect place to relax after a day on the slopes.

🏠 Plaza de San Orencio 3, Vielha 🌐 hotel elciervo.net

€€€

___

Hostal Sa Rascassa
Enjoy personalized service at this gorgeous boutique spot.

🏠 Cala d'Aiguafreda 3, Begur 🌐 hostal saracassa.com

€€€

___

Sant Pere del Bosc
Luxuriate in the lavish suites and spa at this bucolic Modernista villa near the sea.

🏠 Paratge de Sant Pere del Bosc, Lloret de Mar 🌐 sant peredelbosc hotel.com

€€€

___

Mas El Mir
Relax in rustic luxury at this converted farmhouse, set just outside Ripoll.

🏠 Carretera de les Llosses s/n, Ripoll 🌐 maselmir.com

€€€

___

Hotel Horta d'En Rahola
Enjoy the historic setting of this 18th-century manor house within easy reach of the beach.

🏠 Carrer de Sa Tarongeta 1, Cadaqués 🌐 hortacadaques.com

€€€

⑯ Cadaqués

🏛 Girona 🚌 ℹ Carrer Cotxe 1; www.visit cadaques.org

This pretty resort is overlooked by the Baroque Església de Santa Maria. In the 1960s, it was dubbed the "St Tropez of Spain", due to the young crowd that sought out Salvador Dalí in nearby Port Lligat, where he lived for six months of the

↑ A peaceful harbour in Cadaqués, which gets much livelier in summer *(inset)*

year in a fisherman's cabin, from 1930 until his death in 1989. Today the much modified house is known as the **Casa-Museu Salvador Dalí**. Managed by the Gala-Salvador Dalí Foundation, the museum provides a unique interpretation of Dalí's life.

After the museum, head down to the picture-book waterfront, lined with *bodegas*.

Casa-Museu Salvador Dalí

🅿 🏛 Portlligat ⏰ Hours vary, check website (reservations required) 🚫 1 Jan, 7 Jan–early Feb, 25 Dec 🌐 salvador-dali.org

⑰ ♿ Ⓜ Empúries

🏛 Girona 📞 972 77 59 76 🚌 L'Escala ⏰ Mid-Feb–May & Oct: 10am–6pm daily; Jun–Sep: 10am–8pm; mid-Nov–mid-Feb: 10am–5pm 🚫 1 & 6 Jan, 25 Dec

The extensive ruins of this Greco-Roman town occupy an imposing coastal site.

THE ART OF DALÍ

Born in Figueres in 1904, Salvador Dalí mounted his first exhibition at the age of 15. After studying at the Escuela de Bellas Artes in Madrid, and dabbling with Cubism, Futurism and Metaphysical painting, Dalí embraced Surrealism in 1929, becoming the movement's best-known painter. Never far from controversy, self-publicist Dalí became famous for his hallucinatory images, which he described as "hand-painted dream photographs". He died in Figueres in 1989.

Three settlements were built between the 7th and 3rd centuries BC: the old town (Palaiapolis); the new town (Neapolis); and the Roman town. The old town was founded by the Greeks in 600 BC as a trading port. It was built on what was a small island, and is now the site of the tiny hamlet of Sant Martí de Empúries. In 550 BC, this was replaced by a larger new town on the shore that the Greeks named Emporion, meaning "trading place". In 218 BC, the Romans landed at Empúries and built a city next to the new town.

Under the umbrella of the Museu d'Arqueologia de Catalunya *(p132)*, a packed calendar of workshops and events takes place here. Culinary workshops and historical re-enactments introduce children to Roman life. At night, Catalan rock groups and jazz nights are hosted as part of the Concerts in the Forum series.

⑱ Puigcerdà

🏛 Girona 🚍🚌 ℹ Plaça del Santa Maria; www. puigcerda.cat

Puig is Catalan for "hill". And despite sitting on a relatively small hill compared with the encircling mountains – which rise to 2,900 m (9,500 ft) – Puigcerdà nevertheless commands a fine view down into the beautiful Cerdanya valley, the largest in the Pyrenees. The town of Puigcerdà was founded in 1177 by Alfonso II as the capital of Cerdanya, an important agricultural region, which shares a history and culture with the French Cerdagne. The town has links with the Spanish enclave of Llívia, an attractive little town with a medieval pharmacy, which lies 6 km (4 miles) inside France.

Nearby, at the valley's edge, is the mountainous Parc Natural del Cadí-Moixeró, an excellent area laced with trails ideal for ambitious walkers.

---

⑲ Ⓜ Figueres

🏛 Girona 🚍🚌 ℹ Plaça de l'Escorxador 2; www.visit figueres.cat

Figueres is the market town of the Empordà plain, and is perhaps best known as the birthplace of Salvador Dalí, who in 1974 turned the town theatre into the **Teatre-Museu Dalí**. The town's biggest draw is one of the best collections of art by Dalí in the world, housed under the theatre's glass dome, as well as works by a number of other painters. The museum stands as a monument to Catalonia's most eccentric artist, who is also buried here. In the building next door is a permanent collection of flamboyant jewellery that was designed by Dalí between 1941 and 1970.

The third point on the "Dalí Triangle", **Casa-Museu Castell Gala Dalí**, 55 km (35 miles) south of Figueres, is the medieval castle Dalí bought in the 1970s. It contains some of his paintings.

Beyond Dalí, east of Figueres is the Romanesque monastery, Sant Pere de Rodes. On the plane-tree-shaded Rambla is the former Hotel de Paris, now home to the **Museu del Joguet** (Toy Museum). At the bottom of the Rambla is a statue of Narcís Monturiol i Estarriol who, it is believed, invented the submarine.

Teatre-Museu Dalí

♿ 🏛 Plaça Gala-Salvador Dalí 5 🕐 Hours vary, check website 🚫 1 Jan, 25 Dec 🌐 salvador-dali.org

Casa-Museu Castell Gala Dalí

♿♿ 🏛 Carrer de Gala Dalí, Púbol (La Pera) 🕐 Hours vary, check website 🌐 salvador-dali.org

Museu del Joguet

♿ 🏛 Carrer de Sant Pere 1 🕐 Hours vary, check website 🌐 mjc.cat

→

The quirky egg-topped exterior of the Teatre-Museu Dalí in Figueres

TOP 5 WORKS BY DALÍ

The Persistence of Memory, 1931
Perhaps the best known of Dalí's works, these intriguing melting clocks question the meaning of time.

Lobster Telephone, 1936
In this quintessentially Surrealist piece a lobster sits atop a rotary phone.

Metamorphosis of Narcissus, 1927
Dalí's interpretation of the Greek myth of Narcissus through an oil-on-canvas painting.

Swans Reflecting Elephants, 1937
A lake's unusual reflection causes a double-visual of swans and elephants, from Dalí's "Paranoiac-Critical" period.

Galatea of the Spheres, 1952
Spheres show an image of Gala, Dalí's wife and muse.

FLOWERS OF THE MATOLLAR

Furnishing swathes of the eastern Mediterranean coast is the distinctive Catalan *matollar* (matorral). Where once stood forests of holm oak trees, many of which were felled for timber and to provide land for grazing and cultivation, now lies this scrubland landscape blooming with vibrant plants.

Each spring, the *matollar* becomes a kaleidoscope of colourful plants, when hillsides are daubed with yellow broom and pink and white cistuses. The air becomes filled with the scent of aromatic herbs such as rosemary, lavender and thyme, as well as the low drone of insects as they buzz around, feeding on the abundance of nectar and pollen.

All the plants in the *matollar* have adapted to the extremes of climate. They protect themselves from losing water during th dry summer heat with thick leaves or waxy secretions, or by storing moisture in bulbs or tubers.

Several plants from the New World also managed to colonize the bare scrubland ground. The prickly pear, thought to have been brought to Europe by Christopher Columbus, produces a delicious fruit that can be picked only with thickly gloved hands. The century plant, a native of Mexico, thrives in the *matollar's* Mediterranean climate, rapidly erupting from the earth as a splay of tough, spiny green leaves. Only as it approaches the end of its life (10 to 15 years) does it send up a tall flower shoot, after which it dies.

INSIDER TIP
Head to the Hills

Garraf National Park, near Sitges, is a great place to observe the incredible plants and wildlife that Catalonia's *matollar* landscape has to offer, while also enjoying the sea and mountain views. The vegetation typical of the area includes wild olive, Mediterranean fan palm and evergreen oaks. You may also spot rabbits, Mediterranean tortoises and falcons.

Jerusalem Sage

An attractive shrub of greyish-white, woolly leaves, with tall stems surrounded by showy yellow flowers. It's often grown in gardens.

Rose Garlic

This plant has round clusters of violet or pink flowers at the end of a single stalk. It survives the summer as the bulb familiar to all cooks for its strength of flavour.

Spanish Broom

A small bush with yellow flowers on slender branches. The black seed pods split when dry, scattering the seeds on the ground.

Star Clover

This is a low-growing annual whose fruit develops into a star-shaped seed head. Its flowers are often pale pink, or sometimes yellow or purple.

↑ Centauries and St John's worts in bloom in Catalonia

TOP 4 ANIMALS OF THE MATOLLAR

Ladder Snakes
Young ladder snakes are identified by a black pattern like the rungs of a ladder, but adults are marked with two simple stripes.

Scorpions
These venomous predators hide under rocks or wood by day. The scorpions in Catalonia are not deadly to humans, but their sting can pack a punch.

Dartford Warbler
This skulking bird has dark plumage and a cocked tail, and sings melodiously during its mating display. Males are more vividly coloured than females.

Swallowtail Butterfly
One of the most conspicuous insects living in the *matollar*. Its pale yellow wings hemmed with black are unmistakable.

HIDDEN GEM
The Ruins of Ullastret

A short drive from Peratallada are the ruins of this small village, which was once inhabited by an ancient Iberian tribe. Parts of the fascinating ruins date back as far as the 4th century BC.

20
Peratallada

🏠 Girona 🛈 Plaça del Castell 3; www.visit peratallada.cat

This tiny village is the most spectacular of the many that lie a short inland trip from the Costa Brava. Together with Pals and Palau-sator, it forms part of the "Golden Triangle" of medieval villages. Its name is derived from the Catalan for "carved stone", and the village does indeed appear to be cut from the hillside, with its mountaintop position offering dramatic views of the area. A labyrinth of cobbled streets winds up to the well-conserved castle and lookout tower, whose written records date from the 11th century. Peratallada's counts and kings made sure they could fend off any attackers by constructing a sturdy wall enclosing the entire village, which even today limits the nucleus from further expansion.

21
Blanes

🏠 Girona 🚌 🛈 Plaça Catalunya; www.visit blanes.net

The working port of Blanes has one of the longest beaches on the Costa Brava, but the highlight of the town is undoubtedly the **Jardí Botànic Marimurtra**. These gardens, designed by Karl Faust in 1928, are spectacularly sited above cliffs. Their 7,000 species of tropical and Mediterranean plants include African cacti.

Jardí Botànic Marimurtra

🏠 Passeig de Carles Faust 9 🕒 9am–8pm daily 🚫 1 & 6 Jan, 24–26 & 31 Dec 🌐 marimurtra.cat

22
Tossa de Mar

🏠 Girona 🚌 🛈 Avinguda Pelegrí 25; www.info tossa.com

At the end of a tortuous corniche, the Roman town of Turissa is one of the prettiest along the Costa Brava. Above the modern town is the Vila Vella (Old Town), a protected national monument. The medieval walls enclose tidy fishermen's cottages, a 14th-century church and countless bars. The **Museu Municipal** in the old town exhibits local archaeology and modern art.

Museu Municipal

🏠 Plaça Pintor Roig i Soler 1 ☎ 972 34 07 09 🕒 Jun–Sep: 10am–8pm daily; Oct–May: 10am–8pm Tue–Sun

EAT

Sa Capça
Joyful plant-based fare flourishes on the sun-soaked terrace.

🏠 Carrer de Bellaire 4, Blanes 🚫 Tue & Wed

€€€

Compartir
Expert creative plates have earned this spot its Michelin stars.

🏠 Riera de Sant Vicenç, Cadaqués 🚫 Mon 🌐 compartir cadaques.com

€€€

Rafa's
Enjoy informal, mouth-watering, fresh-off-the-boat seafood.

🏠 Carrer de Sant Sebastià 56, Roses ☎ 972 25 40 03

€€€

Cal Sagristà
Head north of Figueres for folksy dishes in a restored old convent.

🏠 Carrer Rodona 2, Peralada ☎ 972 53 83 01

€€€

↑ Twilight settling over the beach in medieval Tossa de Mar

THE "WILD COAST"

A mix of rugged cliffs and sandy beaches, the Costa Brava ("wild coast") runs for some 200 km (125 miles) from Blanes northwards to the region of Empordà, on the border with France.

With its craggy shoreline, pine-backed sandy coves and crowded, modern resorts, the Costa Brava is Spain's answer to the Côte d'Azur. Wine, olives and fishing were the mainstays of the area until the arrival of tourists in the 1960s. They were drawn by some of the finest Blue Flag beaches in Europe, from broad, sandy stretches to horseshoe coves. The busiest resorts are to the south. To the north are quieter fishing villages, while just inland are Roman ruins and medieval villages.

↑ Golden sands and turquoise seas at Aiguablava beach on the Costa Brava

COASTAL RESORT TOWNS

Roses lies at the head of a sweeping bay. Its long, sandy beach has become a mecca for lovers of water sports.

L'Escala, a small resort popular with Spanish tourists, has a series of fine beaches and a small port where fishing nets dry in the sun.

Llafranc, a whitewashed resort with a promenade leading to neighbouring Calella, is one of the coast's most pleasant resorts.

Lloret de Mar has more hotels than anywhere else on the coast. There are some unspoiled beaches nearby, such as Santa Cristina.

Platja d'Aro's long and sandy beach is lined with modern hotels and buzzy beach bars.

The fortified Old Town of Tossa de Mar, flanking either side of its golden beach ↑

SHOP

Llum d'Àngel

This wellness-focused shop is full of soothing scents, gorgeous artisanal candles and appealing natural remedies – balms for the soul.

🏠 Carrer Escasany 32, Cardona 📞 608 42 16 87

Vinum Priorat

Pick from a wide-ranging selection of regional wine and craft beers. There's a small tasting room in the back to sample before you commit to buy.

🏠 Plaça de Catalunya 1, Porrera 🌐 vinum priorat.com

Ceràmica Planas Marquès

Unique ceramics, often crafted from unusual materials, are on sale here. Pieces are offered at reasonable prices, and there's also a workshop attached.

🏠 Avinguda Costa Brava 34, Corçà 🌐 ceramica planasmarques.com

---

23

Sant Pol de Mar

🚉 R1 ℹ️ santpol.cat

This small seaside town is an hour's train ride along the coast from Barcelona on the R1 line; a nice excursion if you're looking to escape the hustle and bustle of the city for a day. A variety of spacious, family-friendly beaches spread out from the centre, all within easy reach of a host of bars and restaurants.

The town once convened around the **Ermita de Sant Pau**, a 10th-century monastery. The remains of this are still standing on a small hill just back from the seafront, and the building also features Romanesque additions dating from the 13th century. A visit to this monastery is worth it for the incredible views alone, but you can also take a look inside the building itself by getting in touch with the local tourist office in advance.

Elsewhere in the town, typically Catalan Modernista architecture can be seen, with the colourfully elaborate **Can Planiol** an especially eye-catching example. Designed by Ignasi Masi Morell and completed in 1910, it is closed to the public, but the captivating façade – sprinkled with ceramic flowers – makes for a great photo opportunity.

No stranger to the Catalan *festa*, the town holds regular festivals throughout the year. In spring, it plays host to Spain's oldest jazz festival, the acclaimed Festival de Jazz de Sant Pol. Towards the end of July, a weekend of celebrations dedicated to Sant Jaume sees the streets come alive with Catalan dancers and *castellers*, and the skies erupt with fireworks. Come September, head to Platja dels Pescadors just up the coast for the popular Festival d'Havaneres. This foodie festival celebrates the humble sardine and the last catch of the season, with barbecues and towering beach bonfires.

Ermita de Sant Pau
🏠 Plaça Sant Pau 2 🕐 On request, apply on website 🌐 santpol.cat

Can Planiol
🏠 Carrer Abat Deas 30 🕐 To the public

24

Cardona

🏠 Barcelona 🚌 ℹ️ Avinguda del Rastrillo; www. cardonaturisme.cat

Situated on a hill near the meandering Riu Cardener is this small historic town, with a Gothic and Romanesque centre that dates back to the 11th century. Its crowning feature is the ancient, ruddy-stoned Castell de Cardona. In the 14th century the castle belonged to the Dukes of Cardona – the most powerful family in Spain besides the royal family itself, who, as constables of Aragón, became known as the "kings without a crown". The castle was rebuilt in the 18th century and is now a luxurious parador. Beside it

←
Whitewashed houses gazing out to sea in pretty Sant Pol de Mar

is an 11th-century church, the handsome Església de Sant Vicenç.

Set on a hill, the castle gives views of the town and of the Muntanya de Sal (Salt Mountain), a huge salt deposit next to the Riu Cardener that has been mined since Roman times. The Muntanya rises 120 m (394 ft) into the air, but even more of its mass is below ground. The mine stretches 2 km (1.2 miles) under the surface; visitors can delve to a depth of 86 m (282 ft) during a tour of the mine.

25

Vic

Barcelona
Plaça del Pes; www.victurisme.cat

Market days are the best time to visit this small country town. This is when the local *embotits* (sausages) for which the area is renowned are piled high in the Gothic Plaça Major, along with other produce from the surrounding plains.

In the 3rd century BC, Vic was the capital of an ancient Iberian tribe, the Ausetans. The town was then colonized by the Romans – the remains of a Roman temple survive today. Since the 6th century, the town has been a bishop's see. In the 11th century, Abbot Oliva commissioned El Cloquer tower, around which the cathedral was built in the 18th century. The interior is covered with vast murals by Josep Maria Sert. Painted in reds and golds, they represent biblical scenes.

Adjacent to the cathedral is the **Museu Episcopal de Vic**, which has one of the best Romanesque collections in Catalonia. The large display of art and relics includes simple murals and wooden carvings from rural churches. Also on display are 11th- and 12th-century frescoes.

↑ Firing up a great hot-air balloon at Vic's Plaça Major

Museu Episcopal de Vic
Plaça Bisbe Oliba 3
May–Aug: 10am–1pm & 3–6pm Tue–Fri, 10am–7pm Sat, 10am–2pm Sun; Sep–Apr: 10am–7pm Tue–Fri, 10am–7pm Sat, 10am–2pm Sun
1 & 6 Jan, 25 & 26 Dec
museuepiscopalvic.com

THE CATALAN LANGUAGE

Catalan has recovered from the ban it suffered under Franco's dictatorship and has supplanted Castilian (Spanish) as the language in everyday use. Spoken by more than 9.5 million people, it is a Romance language akin to the Provençal of France. Suppressed by Felipe V in 1717, Catalan only officially resurfaced in the 19th century, when medieval poetry contests and Catalan literature were revived.

26

Montblanc

Tarragona
Muralla de Santa Tecla 54; www.montblancmedieval.cat

Montblanc's medieval walls are arguably Catalonia's finest example of military architecture. At the Sant Jordi gate, St George allegedly slew the dragon. There is a plaque at the site and an annual festival celebrates this momentous victory. The interesting **Museu Comarcal de la Conca de Barberà** displays local crafts.

Museu Comarcal de la Conca de Barberà
Carrer de Josa 6 977 86 03 49 Summer: 10am-2pm & 4-7pm Tue-Sat, 10am-2pm Sun; Winter: 10am-2pm Tue-Fri & Sun, 10am-2pm & 4-7pm Sat

27

Vilafranca del Penedès

Barcelona **Carrer Hermenegild Clascar 2; 93 818 12 54; www.turismevilafranca.com**

This market town is set in the heart of Penedès, the main wine-producing region of Catalonia. The fascinating **Vinseum** (Wine Museum) documents the history of the area's wine trade and organises tastings every fortnight Local *bodegues* (wineries) can also be visited for wine tasting. Sant Sadurní d'Anoia, the capital of Spain's popular sparkling wine, *cava* *(p200)*, lies just 8 km (5 miles) to the north.

Vinseum
Plaça de Jaume I 10am-2pm, 4-7pm Tue-Sat; 10am-2pm Sun vinmuseum.cat

28

Santes Creus

Tarragona **Plaça Jaume el Just s/n, Monestir; www.larutadelcister.info**

The tiny village of Santes Creus is home to the prettiest of the "Cistercian triangle" monasteries. The other two, Vallbona de les Monges and Poblet, are located nearby. The **Monestir de Santes Creus** was founded in 1150 by Ramon Berenguer IV during his reconquest of Catalonia. The Gothic cloisters are decorated with figurative sculptures, a style first permitted by Jaume II, who ruled from 1291 to 1327. His tomb is in the 12th-century church, which features a rose window.

Monestir de Santes Creus
977 63 83 29 Apr-Sep 10am-7pm, Tue-Sun & public hols; Oct-May 10am-5:30pm, Tue-Sun & public hols 1 & 6 Jan, 25 & 26 Dec

DRINK

Casablanca Cocktail Bar & Art Lounge
Tucked away on a quaint street, this bar offers an excellent cocktail selection and a warm welcome.
Carrer d'en Pau Barrabeig 5, Sitges
93 894 70 82

L'Ombra d'un Sifo
This friendly spot is hung with LP records, and features occasional live music performances.
Riera St 19, Sant Pol de Mar lombradunsifo.blogspot.com

The Blackberry
Perfect for a chilled drink and a chat, this bar has an enviable gin and cocktail selection.
Avinguda Alcalde Rovira Roure 24, Lleida
973 22 56 66

Sputnik Pub
Head to this quirky bar for friendly staff, great drinks - usually served with free tapas - and midnight bingo rounds.
Carrer de Sant Agusti 18b, Solsona
973 48 34 01

The pink-painted 12th-century Monestir de Santes Creus

WINE CATHEDRALS

Catalonia is covered with wineries, and none are more grandiose and spectacular than those designed by Cèsar Martinell. Built with austere reverence to the region's wine heritage, they are known as *les catedrals del vi* (the wine cathedrals).

Cèsar Martinell i Brunet (1888–1973), a protégé of Catalonia's archetypal Modernista architect Antoni Gaudí, was steeped in the Modernista style, though later moved away towards the reactionary Noucentisme. Both styles are represented in his wineries, some of which can be visited today.

His work is typified by finding opulence in his immediate surroundings. He used local materials and traditional techniques to create magnificent buildings that pay homage to the fruits of Catalonia's fertile wine country.

His wine cathedrals are visually reminiscent of their religious counterparts, with arches soaring over large open naves. As well as designing the buildings' structure, he meticulously planned internal layouts, finding balance between practicality and architectural style.

Another Modernista architect, Josep Puig i Cadafalch designed the famous Codorníu winery in Sant Sadurní d'Anoia.

NULLES (1918)

Typically Gaudian Modernista stonework is topped by magnificent pillars of red brick whose varied heights form a roof of sharp peaks and troughs. As well as the striking visual effect, this roof helps regulate the temperature of the winery. Guided group tours can be arranged when booked in advance.

FALSET (1919)

An almost fortress-like white exterior, outlined with red brick and punctuated by arched windows, leads to a large central nave and two adjacent smaller naves, separated by brick pillars and arches. Guided tours are available.

GANDESA (1919)

The naves within this wine cathedral are covered with Catalan vaults; bricks are laid upon an exposed wooden structure, which is itself supported by large brick arches. The smooth, subdued curves of the vaulting lend an unmistakably Modernista style to the unusual roof. The building was extended in 1983 by Manuel Ribas Piera, with respect to the building's original style. Leaflets are handed out for a self-guided tour.

↑ Codorníu's striking façade designed by Josep Puig i Cadafalch

→ The crypt-like cellar beneath the Codorníu winery

The atmospheric beachside town of Sitges, dotted with palm trees ↑

29

Solsona

🏠Lleida 🚌 ℹ️Carretera de Balsell 1, Lleida; www.solsonaturisme.com

Three gateways and nine towers are all that remain of Solsona's fortifications. Inside is an ancient town of noble mansions. The town's cathedral houses a beautiful black stone Virgin. The **Museu Diocesà i Comarcal** contains Romanesque paintings; a wonderfully preserved ice store, the **Pou de Gel**, is also worth a visit.

Museu Diocesà i Comarcal
🏠Plaça del Palau Episcopal 1
📞973 48 21 01 ⏰Hours vary, call ahead 🚫1 & 6 Jan, 25 & 26 Dec

Pou de Gel
♿🚭 🏠Portal del Pont s/n
📞973 48 10 09 ⏰Summer: 6-7:30pm Fri, 11am-12:30pm & 6-7:30pm Sat (to 6:30pm winter); Year-round: 11am-12:30pm Sun

30

Lleida

🏠Lleida 🚇🚌 ℹ️Carretera de Balsell 1; www.turismedelleida.cat

Dominating the capital of Catalonia's only landlocked province is La Suda, a large fort taken from the Moors in 1149. Within its walls stands La Seu Vella, the old cathedral founded in 1203, with a beautiful cloister and Gothic rose window. The well-restored fort complex contains a visitor centre and panoramic viewpoints. The city's **Museu de Lleida** is also a highlight, presenting artifacts that date back to the Stone Age.

Museu de Lleida
♿🚭🕙 🏠Carrer del Sant Crist 1 ⏰Hours vary, check website 🌐museudelleida.cat

> 🔍 HIDDEN GEM
> **Prehistoric Cave Art**
>
> About 30 minutes south of Lleida are the Roca dels Moros (www.mac.es), home to one of the most important collections of Levantine rock art in Iberia. Come here to see a ritual dance daubed in vivid reds some 5,000 years ago.

31

Besalú

🏠Girona 🚌 ℹ️Carrer del Pont 1; www.besalu.cat

A magnificent medieval town with a striking approach across a fortified bridge over the Riu Fluvià, Besalú has two fine Romanesque churches: Sant Vicenç and Sant Pere. The latter is the sole remnant of a Benedictine monastery founded in 977, but pulled down in 1835.

In 1964, a mikvah, a Jewish ritual bath, was discovered by chance. Built in 1264, it is one of only three dating from that period to survive in Europe.

The tourist office has the keys to all the town's attractions.

To the south, the sky-blue lake of Banyoles, where the 1992 Olympic rowing contests were held, is ideal for picnics.

32

Sitges

⌂ Barcelona 🚆🚌 🛈 Plaça Eduard Maristany 2; www. sitgestur.cat

With a lively LGBT+ scene and nine fabulous beaches, Sitges has a reputation as a gay-friendly resort. Buzzy bars and restaurants line its main boulevard, the Passeig Marítim, while Modernista architecture is scattered among the 1970s blocks. Artist Santiago Rusiñol spent much time here and left his quirky collection of art and curios to the **Museu del Cau Ferrat**, at Sebastià beach, next to the 17th-century church of Sant Bartomeu i Santa Tecla.

Museu del Cau Ferrat
♿♻ ⌂ Carrer de Fonollar ☎ 93 894 03 64 🕐 10am–8pm Tue–Sun

←

Walking through the cloister of beautiful La Seu Vella in Lleida

TOP 5 **NIGHT SPOTS IN SITGES**

Pub Voramar
This laid-back pub looks out at the beach.
🕸 www.pub-voramar.com

El Piano
The infectious atmosphere here is fuelled by live performances.
🕸 www.elpianositges.com

El Gin Tub
A classic underground speakeasy with a menu of bespoke gins.
🕸 www.elgintub.com

Bar 7
At this lively bar, punters pick the tunes and fill the dance floor.
☎ 938 94 87 18

Organic
Sitges's original gay-friendly hotspot is still going strong.
☎ 627 53 62 35

←

Flamingos wading in the briny waters of the Delta de L'Ebre

34
Tortosa

◻ Tarragona 🚉 Rambla Felip Pedrell 3; www.tortosaturisme.cat

A ruined castle and medieval walls are clues to Tortosa's historical importance. Sited at the lowest crossing point on the Riu Ebre, it has been strategically significant since Iberian times. The Moors held the city from the 8th century until 1148. The old Moorish castle, known as La Suda, is all

Did You Know?

Castellers climb by holding onto the sashes that each team member wears around his or her waist.

33
Delta de L'Ebre

◻ Tarragona 🚉 Aldea 🚌 Deltebre, Aldea 🛈 Palau Climent, Carrer Montcada 32 3a planta, Tortosa; 🅦 terresdelebre.travel

The delta of the Riu Ebre is a prosperous rice-growing region and wildlife haven. The Parc Natural del Delta de L'Ebre protects a significant water-bird habitat over 70 sq km (27 sq miles). The **Ecomuseu** has an aquarium featuring species found in the delta.

The park is celebrated for its incredible bird watching. Head to the shores of the Punta del Fangar in the north and the Punta de la Banya in the south for the best bird spotting. Here, flamingos breed and can be glimpsed from tourist boats

that leave from Riumar and Deltebre. Amposta and Sant Carles de la Ràpita, the main towns in the area, are good bases for exploring the reserve.

Nearby, up the eastern side of Sierra de Godal, a series of rock shelters house incredible 8,000-year-old cave art. Learn more at the informative **Centro de Interpretación de Arte Rupestre Abrics de la Ermita**.

Ecomuseu

🚸 🕐 ◻ Carrer Doctor Martí Buera 22, Deltebre 📞 977 48 96 79 🕐 10am–1pm & 3–5pm Tue–Sun

Centro de Interpretación de Arte Rupestre Abrics de la Ermita

🚸 🕐 ◻ Ermita de la Pietat, Carretera Ulldecona 📞 977 57 33 94 🕐 Hours vary, call ahead

HUMAN TOWERS

The province of Tarragona is famous for its *casteller* festivals, in which *colles* (groups) of people stand on each other's shoulders in an effort to build the highest human *castell* (tower). Configurations depend on the size of the *colles* who form the base. Teams wear similar colours, and often have names denoting their home town. The small child who has to undertake the perilous climb to the top, where he or she makes the sign of the cross, is called the *anxaneta*. *Castellers* assemble in competition for Tarragona province's major festivals throughout the year. At the end of the tower-building season on St Ursula's Day (21 October), teams from all over Catalonia converge on the town square in Valls.

that remains of their defences. It has now been renovated as a parador. The Moors also built a mosque in Tortosa in 914. Its foundations were used for the present cathedral, on which work began in 1347. Although it was not finished for two centuries, the style is pure Gothic and it can still be visited today in the Old Town. Next to the cathedral is the Palacio Episcopal, begun in the 14th century. Several rooms are open to the public, as is the chapel.

Tortosa was badly damaged in 1938–9 during a fierce Civil War battle, when the Riu Ebre formed the front line between the opposing forces.

35

Costa Daurada

🏠 Tarragona 🚌🚆 Calafell, Sant Vicenç de Calders, Salou 🛈 Passeig de Torroja s/n, Tarragona; www. costadaurada.info

The sandy beaches of the Costa Daurada (Golden Coast) line the shores of Tarragona province. El Vendrell is one of the area's active ports. Nearby, in Sant Salvador, the **Museu Pau Casals** is dedicated to the famous cellist; Casals was born in El Vendrell in 1876, and is buried in the town cemetery.

PortAventura, south of Tarragona, is one of Europe's largest theme parks and has such eclectically themed attractions as Polynesia and Wild West. Ferrari Land has a miniature F1 circuit and the highest, fastest rollercoaster in Europe. Cambrils and Salou to the south are the liveliest resorts – the others are low-key, family holiday spots.

Museu Pau Casals

♿ 🏠 Avinguda Palfuriana 67 📞 902 10 54 64 🕐 10am–2pm & 5–9pm Tue–Sun

PortAventura

♿ 🏠 Avinguda del Batlle Pere Molas Km 2, Vila-seca 📞 902 20 22 20 🕐 Hours vary, call ahead

↓ Crowds thronging through PortAventura on the Costa Daurada

A DRIVING TOUR
CAVA
COUNTRY

Distance 30 km (19 miles) **Stopping-off points**
Masquefa, Sant Sadurní d'Anoia, Vilafranca del Penedès,
Costers del Segre **Difficulty** Best done with a car

Catalonia is the home of cava, Spain's answer to
champagne and one of its most appreciated exports.
Cava country is focused on the Penedès region and
surrounding districts which together make up the
prestigious Penedès DO *(Denominació de Origen)*.
Follow this route through terraced villages, vineyard-
corduroyed countryside and craggy passes with
glinting Mediterranean views. All visits require
booking in advance. You can taste the cavas at each
of the tours, often accompanied by tapas; grape juice
is available instead for those under 18 and the
designated driver.

Did You Know?

Cava was first made in
the mid-19th century
by Josep Raventós,
head of the Codorníu
winery.

↑ Catalonia's countryside, dotted
with picturesque vineyards

La Granada

BP2151

C15

C243A

C15

AP7

Sant Pere
Molanta

N340

In the town of **Vilafranca del**
Penedès *(p194)* find the Mascaró
winery, which offers tours of its cellars.

FINISH
Vilafranca del
Penedès

N340

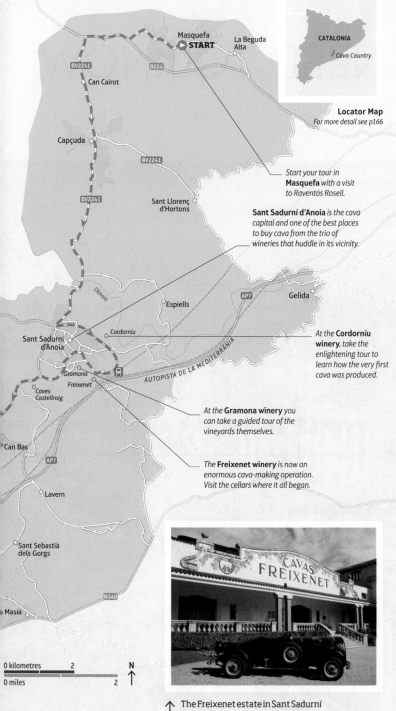

CATALONIA

Cava Country

Locator Map
For more detail see p166

Start your tour in **Masquefa** *with a visit to Raventós Rosell.*

Sant Sadurní d'Anoia *is the cava capital and one of the best places to buy cava from the trio of wineries that huddle in its vicinity.*

At the **Cordorníu winery**, *take the enlightening tour to learn how the very first cava was produced.*

At the **Gramona winery** *you can take a guided tour of the vineyards themselves.*

The **Freixenet winery** *is now an enormous cava-making operation. Visit the cellars where it all began.*

↑ The Freixenet estate in Sant Sadurní d'Anoia, a leading cava producer

0 kilometres   2
0 miles   2

N ↑

NEED TO KNOW

Plaça d'Espanya at sunset

BEFORE
YOU GO

Forward planning is essential to any successful trip. Be prepared for all eventualities by considering the following points before you travel.

AT A GLANCE

CURRENCY
Euro (EUR)

AVERAGE DAILY SPEND

SAVE	SPEND	SPLURGE
€80	€150	€200+

BOTTLED WATER	COFFEE	BEER	DINNER FOR TWO
€0.80	€1	€2.50	€40

SPANISH/CATALAN PHRASES

Hello	Hola/Hola
Goodbye	Adiós/Adéu
Please	Por favor/Si us plau
Thank you	Gracias/Gràcies
Do you speak English	¿Hablas inglés?/ Parles anglès?
I don't understand	No comprendo/ No ho entenc

ELECTRICITY SUPPLY

Power sockets are type F, fitting a two-prong, round-pin plug. Standard voltage is 230 volts.

Passports and Visas

EU nationals may visit for an unlimited period, registering with local authorities after three months. Citizens of the US, Canada, Australia and New Zealand can reside without a visa for up to 90 days. For those arriving from other countries, check with your local Spanish embassy or on the Spanish government's **Exteriores** website.
Exteriores
w exteriores.gob.es

Travel Safety Advice

Get up-to-date travel safety information from the **UK Foreign and Commonwealth Office**, the **US Department of State** and the **Australian Department of Foreign Affairs and Trade.**
Australia
w smartraveller.gov.au
UK
w gov.uk/foreign-travel-advice
US
w travel.state.gov

Customs Information

An individual is permitted to carry the following within the EU for personal use:
Tobacco products 800 cigarettes, 400 cigarillos, 200 cigars or 1 kg of smoking tobacco.
Alcohol 10 litres of alcoholic beverages above 22% strength, 20 litres of alcoholic beverages below 22% strength, 90 litres of wine (60 litres can be sparkling wine) and 110 litres of beer.
Cash If you plan to enter or leave the EU with €10,000 or more in cash (or the equivalent in other currencies), you must declare it to the customs authorities.
Limits vary if travelling outside the EU, so always check restrictions before travelling.

Insurance

It is advisable to take out an insurance policy covering theft, loss of belongings, medical problems, cancellations and delays. EU citizens

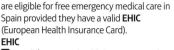

are eligible for free emergency medical care in Spain provided they have a valid **EHIC** (European Health Insurance Card).
EHIC
w gov.uk/european-health-insurance-card

Vaccinations

No inoculations are necessary for Spain.

Money

Most urban establishments accept major credit, debit and prepaid currency cards. Contactless payments are common in cities, but it's a good idea to carry cash for smaller items. ATMs are widely available around the country, although many charge for cash withdrawals.

Booking Accommodation

Catalonia offers a range of accommodation, including a government-run hotels called paradors. A useful list of accommodation can be found on the **Turespaña** website.

Try to book your accommodation well in advance if you plan to visit in the peak season (July and August). Rates are also higher during major fiestas.

Most hotels quote prices without including tax (IVA), which is 10 per cent. In Barcelona, visitors must pay a nightly tax that varies from 75¢ to €2.50 depending on the number of stars of the hotel. There is a seven-day maximum.
Turespaña
w spain.info

Travellers with Specific Needs

Spain's **COCEMFE** (Confederación Española de Personas con Discapacidad Física y Orgánica) and **Accessible Spain** provide useful information, while companies, such as **Tourism For All**, offer specialist tours for those with reduced mobility, sight and hearing.

Spain's public transport system generally caters for all passengers, with wheelchairs, adapted toilets, and reserved car parking available at airports and stations. Trains and some buses accommodate wheelchair-bound passengers. Metro maps in Braille are available from **ONCE** (Organización Nacional de Ciegos).

Accessible Spain
w accessiblespaintravel.com
COCEMFE
w cocemfe.es
Tourism For All
w tourismforall.org.uk
ONCE
w once.es

Language

The two official languages of Catalonia are *castellano* (Castilian Spanish) and Catalan. Almost every Catalan can speak Castilian Spanish, but most consider Catalan their first language. As a visitor, it is perfectly acceptable to speak Castilian wherever you are. English is widely spoken in the cities and other tourist spots, but not always in rural areas.

Closures

Lunchtime Many shops and some museums and public buildings may close for the siesta, roughly between 1pm and 5pm.
Monday Many museums, public buildings and monuments are closed all day.
Sunday Churches and cathedrals are closed to the public during Mass. Some public transport runs less frequently.
Public holidays Most museums, public buildings and many shops close early or for the day.

PUBLIC HOLIDAYS

1 Jan	New Year's Day
6 Jan	Three Kings' Day
19 Apr	Good Friday
22 Apr	Easter Monday
1 May	Labour Day
10 Jun	Pentecost
24 Jun	Sant Joan
15 Aug	The Assumption
11 Sep	Catalan National Day
12 Oct	Spain's National Day
1 Nov	All Saints' Day
6 Dec	Spanish Constitution Day
8 Dec	Feast of the Immaculate Conception
25 Dec	Christmas Day
26 Dec	Boxing Day

GETTING
AROUND

Whether you are visiting for a short city break or rural country retreat, discover how best to reach your destination and travel like a pro.

AT A GLANCE

PUBLIC TRANSPORT COSTS

METRO

€2.20

Single-ride ticket

BUS

€2.20

Single-ride ticket

METRO, BUS, LOCAL TRAINS

€8.60

All-day travel ticket

These prices listed here are for travel within Zone 1.

SPEED LIMIT

MOTORWAY

120 km/h (75mph)

DUAL CARRIAGEWAYS

100 km/h (60mph)

SECONDARY ROAD

90 km/h (55mph)

URBAN AREAS

50 km/h (30mph)

Arriving by Air

Barcelona's international airport, the El Prat Josep Tarradellas, is 16 km (10 miles) west of the city. European budget airlines fly to Barcelona all year round. There are regular internal flights to local airports: Sabadell Airport, 20 km (12 miles) north of Barcelona, Lleida–Alguaire Airport, Reus Airport in Tarragona, Girona–Costa Brava Airport and Andorra–La Seu d'Urgell Airport.

For information on getting to and from Barcelona's airport, see the table opposite.

Barcelona El Prat Josep Tarradellas
W aeropuertobarcelona-elprat.com

Train Travel

International Train Travel

Spain's rail services are operated by state-run **Renfe** (Red Nacional de Ferrocarriles Españoles). Buy your ticket on their website well ahead of travel, particularly for the peak summer season.

There are several routes to Spain from France. Trains from London, Brussels, Amsterdam, Geneva, Zürich and Milan reach Barcelona via Cerbère, on the French border with Catalonia. Direct, high-speed luxury TALGO (Tren Articulado Ligero Goicoechea Oriol) trains, operated by Renfe, go to Barcelona from Paris, Milan, Geneva and Zürich. International trains arrive at Barcelona's Sants mainline station.

Renfe
W renfe.com

Domestic Train Travel

Renfe is the national rail operator, from whom you can buy tickets online or at the station.

The fastest intercity services are the TALGO and AVE (operated by Renfe), which link Madrid with Barcelona in three hours. AVE routes link Barcelona with Seville and Málaga in five and a half hours. The *largo recorrido* (long-distance) trains are cheap but so slow that you usually need to travel overnight. *Regionales y cercanías* (regional and local services) are frequent and cheap. Overnight trains are offered by Estrella (a basic service) to Madrid, and by Trenhotel (more sophisticated) to A Coruña and Vigo, in Galicia.

GETTING TO AND FROM THE AIRPORT

Airport	Transport to Centre	Price	Journey Time
Barcelona El Prat Josep Tarradellas	taxi	€25-32	20 mins
(Terminals 1 & 2)	Aerobús	€5.90	35 mins
(Terminals 1 & 2)	metro	€4.60	45 mins
(Terminal 2)	local train	€2.20	30 mins

CAR JOURNEY PLANNER

Plotting the main driving routes according to journey time, this map is a handy reference for travelling between Spain's main cities by car. The times given reflect the fastest and most direct routes available. Tolls apply on *autopistas* motorways but not on *autovías*.

A Coruña
Santiago de Compostela
Bilbao
Girona
Zaragoza
Barcelona
Tarragona
Madrid
Valencia
Seville
Murcia
Granada
Málaga
Cadiz

Barcelona to Girona	2.5 hrs	**Madrid to Málaga**	5.5 hrs
Barcelona to Tarragona	1.25 hrs	**Madrid to Murcia**	4 hrs
Barcelona to Valencia	4 hrs	**Madrid to Santiago de Compostela**	6.5 hrs
Barcelona to Zaragoza	3.5 hrs	**Madrid to Seville**	5.5 hrs
Bilbao to Zaragoza	3 hrs	**Madrid to Valencia**	3.75 hrs
Málaga to Granada	1.5 hrs	**Madrid to Zaragoza**	3 hrs
Málaga to Murcia	4.5 hrs	**Santiago de Compostela to A Coruña**	1 hr
Málaga to Seville	2.5 hrs	**Seville to Cadiz**	1.5 hrs
Madrid to Barcelona	6 hrs	**Seville to Granada**	2.75 hrs
Madrid to Bilbao	4.25 hrs	**Valencia to Murcia**	2.5 hrs

Long-Distance Bus Travel

Often the cheapest way to reach and travel around Spain is by coach. **Eurolines** runs daily services to Barcelona's Sants bus station.

Spain has no national coach company; private regional companies operate routes around the country. The largest is **Alsa**, with routes and services covering most of Spain. Tickets and information are available at all main coach stations and on company websites.

Buses from towns and cities in Spain arrive at Estació del Nord and Sants. Several companies run day trips or longer tours around Catalonia. **Turisme de Catalunya** has details of trips.

Alsa
W alsa.es
Eurolines
W eurolines.com
Turisme de Catalunya
W catalunyaturisme.cat

Public Transport

Most towns and cities in Catalonia only offer a bus service, but the larger cities operate multiple public transport systems, including trams. Barcelona, **Girona**, **Tarragona** and **Lleida** all have cheap and efficient bus services. Barcelona also has a well-run metro system. For up-to-date information about public transport, as well as ticket advice, check out municipal websites.

Metro maps are available at stations. Bus maps are available at the bigger tourist offices. Both are available through **TMB** (Transports Metropolitans de Barcelona), which has a useful interactive website, as well as an app.

A range of tickets and money-saving travel cards are available to tourists. Some cover train, bus and metro. Combined tickets allow you to hop from metro to FGC to bus lines without having to pay again. The *senzill* ticket, for a single journey, is €2.20 and can be used on metro, bus and FGC; the T-10 is €10.20, can be shared and is the most useful for tourists, allowing ten trips on metro, bus and FGC (these can be combined with a time limit of an hour and a half); T-Dia and T-Mes are for unlimited daily and monthly travel respectively; the T-50/30 is for 50 journeys in 30 days on metro, bus and FGC.

For tourists, there are two-, three-, four- and five-day Hola Barcelona travel cards available (€15.20, €22.20, €28.80 and €35.40 if bought online through TMB) – these offer unlimited journeys on the metro, FGC and bus. Hola Barcelona cards also include the metro supplement for trips to and from the airport.

Girona
W girona.cat
Lleida
W atmlleida.cat

Tarragona
W tarragonaturisme.cat
TMB
W tmb.cat

Metro

There are 12 underground metro lines in Barcelona, run by TMB. Lines are identified by number and colour. Platform signs distinguish between trains and their direction by displaying the last station on the line. In the street, look for a sign bearing a red "M" on a white diamond background. The metro is usually the quickest way to get around the city, especially as all multi-journey tickets are valid for the metro and FGC lines (in Zone 1), as well as on the bus and local RENFE services. A RENFE or FGC sign at a metro station indicates that it has a RENFE or FGC connection. Metro trains run from 5am to midnight from Monday to Thursday, to midnight on Sunday and weekday public holidays, from 5am to 2am on Friday and the day before a public holiday, and all night on Saturdays.

The L9 metro line connects the city with the airport, and it stops at terminals 1 and 2, but is only really useful if you are headed to the north or west of the city. An airport supplement is charged on this route, and you will not be able to use the T-10 or other standard transport passes. However, the Hola Barcelona pass includes the airport supplement and is accepted on this route.

Trams

Barcelona has comprehensive tram networks. This is a cheap and efficient way to travel, and trams are often more accessible than other modes of public transport for those with limited mobility or travelling with pushchairs.

Bus

Buses are the most common mode of public transport in Catalonia, but timetables can be erratic. Many services do not run after 10pm, but there are some night buses in the cities.

In Barcelona the T-10 and T-2Dies tickets are valid on buses and trams, on the metro and on trains to the airport. The main city buses are white and red. Bus numbers beginning with H (for horizontal) run from one side of the city to another and those beginning with V (vertical) run top to bottom; D is diagonal. The Nitbus service runs nightly from around 10:30pm to 5am. Excellent bus maps are available from the main tourist office in Plaça de Catalunya.

The privately owned **Aerobús** runs between Plaça de Catalunya and El Prat airport. Public transport passes are not valid on the Aerobús.

Aerobús
W aerobusbcn.com

NEED TO KNOW Getting Around

Local Trains

RENFE's network of local trains, *cercanías,* is useful for longer distances within Barcelona, particularly between the main train stations: Sants and Estació de França. They are also useful for short hops to Sitges or the northern coastal towns. Maps are displayed at stations, or are available on the RENFE website. Trains run 5:30am to 11:30pm daily, but hours vary from line to line. **Ferrocarrils de la Generalitat de Catalunya (FGC)** is a network of suburban trains run by the Catalan Government in and around Barcelona. They are useful for trips to Tibidabo, Pedralbes and the Collserola neighbourhoods.

Ferrocarrils de la Generalitat de Catalunya (FGC)
W fgc.cat

Taxis

Barcelona's taxis are yellow and black, displaying a green light when free. All taxis are metered and show a minimum fee at the start of a journey. Generally speaking, the journey starts with a flat fee and then increases depending on the distance travelled. Rates increase between 8pm and 8am, and there is a €2.10 surcharge from midnight to 6am Friday to Sunday and on public holidays. Surcharges usually apply for going to and from the airport, the port and major train stations. You can flag taxis in the street, or call **Radio Taxis** to order one. **Taxi Amic** has cars adapted for people with a disability, though these need to be booked a day ahead.

Radio Taxis
W radiotaxibarcelona.info
Taxi Amic
W taxi-amic-adaptat.com

Driving

If you drive to Spain in your own car, you must carry the vehicle's registration document, a valid insurance certificate, a passport or a national identity card and your driving licence at all times. You must also display a sticker on the back of the car showing its country of registration.

Spain has two types of motorway: *autopistas,* (toll roads) and *autovías* (toll-free). You can establish whether a motorway is toll-free by the letters that prefix the number of the road: A = free motorway, AP = toll motorway.

Carreteras nacionales, Spain's main roads, have black-and-white signs and are designated by the letter N (Nacional) plus a number. *Carreteras comarcales,* secondary roads, have a number preceded by the letter C.

Parking in Barcelona can be difficult. The city has a pay-and-display system from 9am to 2pm and 4pm to 8pm Monday to Friday and all day Saturday. You can park in blue spaces for about €2–3 per hour. Tickets are valid for 2 hours but can be renewed. Green spaces are reserved for residents but can be used, if available, at a higher rate and are free at off-peak hours. At underground car parks, *lliure* means there is space, *complet* means full. Most are attended, but in automatic ones, you pay before returning to your car. Do not park where the pavement edge is yellow or where there is a private exit (*gual*). Blue and red signs saying "1–15" or "16–30" mean that you cannot park in the areas indicated on those dates of the month.

Driving to Barcelona

Many people drive to Catalonia via France. The most direct routes across the Pyrenees are the motorways through Hendaye in the west and La Jonquera in the east. Port Bou is on a coastal route, while other routes snake over the top, entering Catalonia via the Val d'Aran, Andorra and Puigcerdà in the Cerdanya. From the UK, car ferries run from Plymouth to Santander and from Portsmouth to Santander and Bilbao.

Car Rental

The most popular car-rental companies are **Avis, Europcar** and **Hertz.** All have offices at airports, major train stations and in the larger cities.

Avis
W avis.com
Europcar
W europcar.com
Hertz
W hertz-europe.com

Rules of the Road

Most traffic regulations and warnings to motorists are represented on signs by easily recognized symbols. To turn left at a busy junction or across oncoming traffic, you may have to turn right first and cross a main road, often by way of traffic lights, a bridge or underpass. If you are accidentally going in the wrong direction on a motorway or a main road with a solid white line, turn round at a sign for a *cambio de sentido*. At crossings, give way to the right unless a sign indicates otherwise.

Cycling

Barcelona has a number of cycle-hire shops and a growing network of cycle lanes that provide access to all the major sights of the city. **Bicing**, the municipal government-run free service, can be used with a Bicing card and supplies maps of the city's cycle lanes. Though this is currently open to residents only, commercial operators offer rentals to visitors from around €10 for two hours to €60 for a week.

Bicing
W bicing.barcelona

PRACTICAL
INFORMATION

A little local know-how goes a long way in Barcelona. Here you will find all the essential advice and information you will need during your stay.

AT A GLANCE

EMERGENCY NUMBERS

EMERGENCY
OPERATOR

112

TIME ZONE
CET/CEST: Central European Summer time (CEST) runs from the last Sunday in March to the last Sunday in October.

TAP WATER
Tap water in Spain is safe to drink unless stated otherwise.

TIPPING

Waiter	5-10 per cent
Hotel Porter	€1-2 per bag
Housekeeping	Not expected
Concierge	Not expected
Taxi Driver	Round up to nearest euro

Personal Security

Violent crime is rare in Spain, but visitors should avoid walking alone in poorly lit areas. Take particular care at markets, tourist sights and stations, and wear bags and cameras across your body, not on your shoulder. Be especially careful of pickpockets when getting on or off a crowded train or metro. Contact your embassy if you have your passport stolen, or in the event of a serious crime or accident.

Health

Seek medicinal supplies and advice for minor ailments from a pharmacy *(farmacia),* identifiable by a green or red cross. Pharmacists can dispense a range of drugs that would normally be available only on prescription in many other countries. Each pharmacy displays a card in the window showing the address of the nearest all-night pharmacy.

Emergency medical care in Spain is free for all EU citizens. If you have an EHIC *(p204),* present this as soon as possible. You may have to pay after treatment and reclaim the money later.

For visitors coming from outside the EU, payment of hospital and other medical expenses is the patient's responsibility, so it is important to arrange comprehensive medical insurance before travelling.

Smoking, Alcohol and Drugs

Smoking is banned in enclosed public spaces and is a fineable offence, although you can still smoke on the terraces of bars and restaurants.

Spain has a relaxed attitude towards alcohol consumption, but it is frowned upon to be openly drunk. In cities it is common to drink on the street outside the bar of purchase.

Most recreational drugs are illegal, and possession of even a very small quantity can lead to an extremely hefty fine. Amounts that suggest an intent to supply drugs to other people can lead to custodial sentences. Cannabis clubs can supply the drug to members, but it remains illegal to smoke it in public spaces.

ID

By law you must carry identification with you at all times in Spain. A photocopy of your passport should suffice. If stopped by the police, you may be asked to report to a police station with the original document.

Local Customs

Regional pride is strong throughout Spain. Be wary of referring to Catalans as "Spanish", as this can sometimes cause offence.

A famous Spanish tradition is the siesta, which sees many shops closing between 1pm and 5pm. This is not always observed by large stores or in very touristy areas.

Visiting Churches and Cathedrals

Most churches and cathedrals will not permit visitors during Sunday Mass. Generally, entrance to churches is free, however a fee may apply to enter special areas, like cloisters.

It is wise to ensure that you are dressed modestly when visiting religious buildings, with knees and shoulders covered.

Mobile Phones and Wi-Fi

Free Wi-Fi is reasonably common, particularly in libraries, large public spaces, restaurants and bars. Some places, such as airports and hotels, may charge for using their Wi-Fi. Barcelona City Council provides free Wi-Fi throughout much of the city centre, but bandwidth is very limited.

Visitors travelling to Spain with EU tariffs can use their devices abroad without being affected by roaming charges. Users will be charged the same rates for data, calls and texts as at home.

Post

Correos is Spain's postal service. Mail sent within the same city usually takes a day to arrive. Deliveries between cities take two to three days. Urgent or important post can be sent by *urgente* (express) or *certificado* (registered) mail. For fast delivery, use the Correos Postal Express Service or a private courier.

Stamps can be purchased from a post office, a *papelería* (stationery shop) or an *estanco* (tobacconist). Postal rates fall into three price bands: Spain; Europe and North Africa; and the rest of the world. Parcels must be weighed and stamped at Correos offices.

Letters sent from a post office usually arrive more quickly than if posted in a *buzón* (postbox). In cities, postboxes are yellow pillar boxes; elsewhere they are wall-mounted postboxes.

Correos
W correos.es

Taxes and Refunds

IVA (VAT) is normally 21 per cent, but with lower rates for certain goods and services, such as restaurants and hotels. Under certain conditions, non-EU citizens can claim a rebate of these taxes. Retailers can give you a form to fill out, which you can then present to a customs officer with your receipts as you leave. If the shop offers DIVA, you can fill that form out instead and validate it automatically at self-service machines found in the airport.

Discount Cards

Barcelona offers the **Barcelona Card**, a visitor's pass or discount card for exhibitions, events and museum entry, plus participating restaurants. This is not free, so consider carefully how many of the offers you are likely to take advantage of before purchasing a card.

Barcelona Card
W barcelonacard.org

WEBSITES AND APPS

Visit Barcelona
The city's website for tourists (www.barcelonaturisme.com)

Catalunya Turisme
Catalonia's official tourism website (www.catalunyaturisme.cat)

Moovit
A route-planning app that includes public transport

WiFi Map
Available as a website and an app, it finds free Wi-Fi hotspots near you (www.wifimap.io)

INDEX

Index

CATALAN PHRASE BOOK

IN EMERGENCY

Help!	Auxili!	ow-gzee-lee
Stop!	Pareu!	pah-reh-oo
Call a doctor!	Telefoneu un metge!	teh-leh-fon-eh-oo oon meh-djuh
Call an ambulance!	Telefoneu una ambulància!	teh-leh-fon-eh-oo oo-nah ahm-boo-lahn-see-ah
Call the police!	Telefoneu la policia!	teh-leh-fon-eh-oo lah poh-lee-see-ah
Call the fire brigade!	Telefoneu els bombers!	teh-leh-fon-eh-oo uhlz boom-behs
Where is the nearest telephone?	On és el telèfon més proper?	on-ehs uhl tuh-leh-fon mehs proo-peh
Where is the nearest hospital?	On és l'hospital més proper?	on-ehs looss-pee-tahl mehs proo-peh

COMMUNICATION ESSENTIALS

Yes	Sí	see
No	No	noh
Please	Si us plau	sees plah-oo
Thank you	Gràcies	grah-see-uhs
Excuse me	Perdoni	puhr-thoh-nee
Hello	Hola	oh-lah
Goodbye	Adéu	ah-they-oo
Good night	Bona nit	bo-nah neet
Morning	El matí	uhl muh-tee
Afternoon	La tarda	lah tahr-thuh
Evening	El vespre	uhl vehs-pruh
Yesterday	Ahir	ah-ee
Today	Avui	uh-voo-ee
Tomorrow	Demà	duh-mah
Here	Aquí	uh-kee
There	Allà	uh-lyah
What?	Què?	keh
When?	Quan?	kwahn
Why?	Per què?	puhr keh
Where?	On?	ohn

USEFUL PHRASES

How are you?	Com està?	kom uhs-tah
Very well, thank you.	Molt bé, gràcies.	mol beh grah-see-uhs
Pleased to meet you.	Molt de gust.	mol duh goost
See you soon.	Fins aviat.	feenz uhv-yat
That's fine.	Està bé.	uhs-tah beh
Where is/are ...?	On és/són?	ohn ehs/sohn
How far is it to ...?	Quants metres/ kilòmetres hi ha d'aquí a ...?	kwahnz meh-truhs/ kee-loh-muh-truhs yah dah-kee uh
Which way to ...?	Per on es va a ...?	puhr on uhs bah ah
Do you speak English?	Parles anglès?	par-luhs an-glehs
I don't understand.	No l'entenc.	noh luhn-teng
Could you speak more slowly, please?	Pot parlar més a poc a poc, si us plau?	pot par-lah mehs pok uh pok sees plah-oo
I'm sorry.	Ho sento.	oo sehn-too

USEFUL WORDS

big	gran	gran
small	petit	puh-teet
hot	calent	kah-len
cold	fred	fred
good	bo	boh
bad	dolent	doo-len
enough	bastant	bahs-tan
well	bé	beh
open	obert	oo-behr
closed	tancat	tan-kat
left	esquerra	uhs-kehr-ruh
right	dreta	dreh-tuh
straight on	recte	rehk-tuh
near	a prop	uh prop
far	lluny	lyoonyuh
up/over	a dalt	uh dahl
down/under	a baix	uh bah-eeshh
early	aviat	uhv-yat
late	tard	tahrt
entrance	entrada	uhn-trah-thuh
exit	sortida	soor-tee-thuh

toilet	lavabos/ serveis	luh-vah-boos sehr-beh-ees
more	més	mess
less	menys	menyees

SHOPPING

How much does this cost?	Quant costa això?	kwahn kost ehs-shoh
I would like ...	M'agradaria ...	muh-grad-uh-ree-ah
Do you have?	Tenen?	tehn-un
I'm just looking, thank you.	Només estic mirant, gràcies.	noo-mess ehs-teek mee-rahn grah-see-uhs
Do you take credit cards?	Accepten targes de crèdit?	ak-sehp-tuhn tahr-zhuhs duh kreh-deet
What time do you open?	A quina hora obren?	ah keen-uh oh-ruh oh-bruhn
What time do you close?	A quina hora tanquen?	ah keen-uh oh-ruh tan-kuhn
This one.	Aquest	ah-ket
That one.	Aquell	ah-kehl
expensive	car	kahr
cheap	bé de preu/ barat	beh thuh preh-oo/ bah-rat
size (clothes)	talla/mida	tah-lyah/mee-thuh
size (shoes)	número	noo-mehr-oo
white	blanc	blang
black	negre	neh-gruh
red	vermell	vuhr-mel
yellow	groc	grok
green	verd	behrt
blue	blau	blah-oo
antique store	antiquari/botiga d'antiguitats	on-tee-kwah-ree/ boo-tee-gah/dan-tee-ghee-tats
bakery	el forn	uhl forn
bank	el banc	uhl bang
book store	la llibreria	lah lyee-bruh-ree-ah
butcher's	la carnisseria	lah kahr-nee-suh-ree-uh
pastry shop	la pastisseria	lah pahs-tee-suh-ree-uh
chemist's	la farmàcia	lah fuhr-mah-see-ah
fishmonger's	la peixateria	lah peh-shuh-tuh-ree-uh
greengrocer's	la fruiteria	lah froo-ee-tuh-ree-uh
grocer's	la botiga de queviures	lah boo-tee-guh duh keh-vee-oo-ruhs
hairdresser's	la perruqueria	lah peh-roo-kuh-ree-uh
market	el mercat	uhl muhr-kat
newsagent's	el quiosc de premsa	uhl kee-ohsk duh prem-suh
post office	l'oficina de correus	loo-fee-see-nuh duh koo-reh-oos
shoe store	la sabateria	lah sah-bah-tuh-ree-uh
supermarket	el supermercat	uhl soo-puhr-muhr-kat
tobacconist's	l'estanc	luhs-tang
travel agency	l'agència de viatges	la-jen-see-uh duh vee-ad-juhs

SIGHTSEEING

art gallery	la galeria d' art	lah gah-luh-ree-yuh dart
cathedral	la catedral	lah kuh-tuh-thrahl
church	l'església la basílica	luhz-gleh-zee-uh lah buh-zee-lee-kuh
garden	el jardí	uhl zhahr-dee
library	la biblioteca	lah bee-blee-oo-teh-kuh
museum	el museu	uhl moo-seh-oo
tourist information office	l'oficina de turisme	loo-fee-see-nuh thuh too-reez-muh
town hall	l'ajuntament	luh-djoon-tuh-men
closed for holiday	tancat per vacances	tan-kat puh bah-kan-suhs
bus station	l'estació d'autobusos	luhs-tah-see-oh dow-toh-boo-zoos
railway station	l'estació de tren	luhs-tah-see-oh thuh tren

STAYING IN A HOTEL

Do you have a vacant room?	¿Tenen una habitació lliure?	*teh-nuhn oo-nuh ah-bee-tuh-see-oh lyuh-ruh*
double room with double bed	habitació doble amb llit de matrimoni	*ah-bee-tuh-see-oh doh-bluh am lyeet duh mah-tree-moh-nee*
twin room	habitació amb dos llits/ amb llits individuals	*ah-bee-tuh-see-oh am dohs lyeets/ am lyeets in-thee-vee-thoo-ahls*
single room	habitació individual	*ah-bee-tuh-see-oh een-dee-vee-thoo-ahl*
room with a bath	habitació amb bany	*ah-bee-tuh-see-oh am bah-nyuh*
shower	dutxa	*doo-chuh*
porter	el grum	*uhl groom*
key	la clau	*lah klah-oo*
I have a reservation.	Tinc una habitació reservada.	*ting oo-nuh ah-bee-tuh-see-oh reh-sehr-vah-thah*

EATING OUT

Have you got a table for...	Tenen taula per...?	*teh-nuhn tow-luh puhr*
I would like to reserve a table.	Voldria reservar una taula.	*vool-dree-uh reh-sehr-vahr oo-nuh tow-luh*
The bill please.	El compte, si us plau.	*uhl kohm-tuh sees plah-oo*
I am a vegetarian.	Sóc vegetarià.	*sok buh-zhuh-tuh-ree-ah*
waitress	cambrera	*kam-breh-ruh*
waiter	cambrer	*kam-breh*
menu	la carta	*lah kahr-tuh*
fixed-price menu	menú del migdia	*muh-noo thuhl midge dee-uh*
wine list	la carta de vins	*lah kahr-tuh thuh veens*
glass of water	un got d'aigua	*oon got dah-ee-gwah*
glass of wine	una copa de vi	*oo-nuh ko-pah thuh vee*
bottle	una ampolla	*oo-nuh am-pol-yuh*
knife	un ganivet	*oon gun-ee-veht*
fork	una forquilla	*oo-nuh foor-keel-yuh*
spoon	una cullera	*oo-nuh kool-yeh-ruh*
breakfast	l'esmorzar	*les-moor-sah*
lunch	el dinar	*uhl dee-nah*
dinner	el sopar	*uhl soo-pah*
main course	el primer plat	*uhl pree-meh plat*
starters	els entrants	*uhlz ehn-tranz*
dish of the day	el plat del dia	*uhl plat duhl dee-uh*
coffee	el cafè	*uhl kah-feh*
rare	poc fet	*pok fet*
medium	al punt	*ahl poon*
well done	molt fet	*mol fet*

MENU DECODER

l'aigua mineral	*lah-ee-gwuh mee-nuh-rahl*	mineral water
sense gas/ amb gas	*sen-zuh gas/ am gas*	still/ sparkling
al forn	*ahl forn*	baked
l'all	*lahl yuh*	garlic
l'arròs	*lahr-roz*	rice
les botifarres	*lahs boo-tee-fah-rahs*	sausages
la carn	*lah karn*	meat
la ceba	*lah seh-buh*	onion
la cervesa	*lah-sehr-ve-sah*	beer
l'embotit	*lum-boo-teet*	cold meat
el filet	*uhl fee-let*	sirloin
el formatge	*uhl for-mah-djuh*	cheese
fregit	*freh-zheet*	fried
la fruita	*lah froo-ee-tah*	fruit
els fruits secs	*uhlz froo-eets seks*	nuts
les gambes	*lahs gam-bus*	prawns
el gelat	*uhl djuh-lat*	ice cream
la llagosta	*lah lyah-gos-tuh*	lobster
la llet	*lah lyet*	milk
la llimona	*lah lyee-moh-nah*	lemon
la llimonada	*lah lyee-moh-nah-thuh*	lemonade
la mantega	*lah mahn-teh-gah*	butter
el marisc	*uhl mah-reesk*	seafood
la menestra	*lah muh-nehs-truh*	vegetable stew
l'oli	*loll-ee*	oil
les olives	*luhs oo-lee-vuhs*	olives
l'ou	*loh-oo*	egg
el pa	*uhl pah*	bread

el pastís	*uhl pahs-tees*	pie/cake
les patates	*lahs pah-tah-tuhs*	potatoes
el pebre	*uhl peh-bruh*	pepper
el peix	*uhl pehsh*	fish
el pernil salat serrà	*uhl puhr-neel suh-lat sehr-rah*	cured ham
el plàtan	*uhl plah-tun*	banana
el pollastre	*uhl poo-lyah-struh*	chicken
la poma	*la poh-mah*	apple
el porc	*uhl pohr*	pork
les postres	*lahs pohs-truhs*	dessert
rostit	*rohs-teet*	roast
la sal	*lah sahl*	salt
la salsa	*lah sahl-suh*	sauce
les salsitxes	*lahs sahl-see-chuhs*	sausages
sec	*sehk*	dry
la sopa	*lah soh-puh*	soup
el sucre	*uhl-soo-kruh*	sugar
la taronja	*lah tuh-rohn-djuh*	orange
el te	*uhl teh*	tea
les torrades	*lahs too-rah-thuhs*	toast
la vedella	*lah veh-theh-lyuh*	beef
el vi blanc	*uhl bee blang*	white wine
el vi negre	*uhl bee neh-gruh*	red wine
el vi rosat	*uhl bee roo-zaht*	rosé wine
el vinagre	*uhl bee-nah-gruh*	vinegar
el xai/el be	*uhl shahee/uhl beh*	lamb
el xerès	*uhl shuh-rehs*	sherry
la xocolata	*lah shoo-koo-lah-tuh*	chocolate
el xoriç	*uhl shoo-rees*	red sausage

NUMBERS

0	zero	*seh-roo*
1	un (masc)/una (fem)	*oon/oon-uh*
2	dos (masc)/dues (fem)	*dohs/doo-uhs*
3	tres	*trehs*
4	quatre	*kwa-truh*
5	cinc	*seeng*
6	sis	*sees*
7	set	*set*
8	vuit	*voo-eet*
9	nou	*noh-oo*
10	deu	*deh-oo*
11	onze	*on-zuh*
12	doce	*doh-dzuh*
13	tretze	*treh-dzuh*
14	catorze	*kah-tohr-dzuh*
15	quinze	*keen-zuh*
16	setze	*set-zuh*
17	disset	*dee-set*
18	divuit	*dee-voo-eet*
19	dinou	*dee-noh-oo*
20	vint	*been*
21	vint-i-un	*been-tee-oon*
22	vint-i-dos	*been-tee-dohs*
30	trenta	*tren-tah*
31	trenta-un	*tren-tah oon*
40	quaranta	*kwuh-ran-tuh*
50	cinquanta	*seen-kwahn-tah*
60	seixanta	*seh-ee-shan-tah*
70	setanta	*seh-tan-tah*
80	vuitanta	*voo-ee-tan-tah*
90	noranta	*noh-ran-tah*
100	cent	*sen*
101	cent un	*sent oon*
102	cent dos	*sen dohs*
200	dos-cents (masc) dues-centes (fem)	*dohs-sens doo-uhs sen-tuhs*
300	tres-cents	*trehs-sens*
400	quatre-cents	*kwah-truh-senz*
500	cinc-cents	*seeng-senz*
600	sis-cents	*sees-senz*
700	set-cents	*set-senz*
800	vuit-cents	*voo-eet-senz*
900	nou-cents	*noh-oo-cenz*
1,000	mil	*meel*
1,001	mil un	*meel oon*

TIME

one minute	un minut	*oon mee-noot*
one hour	una hora	*oo-nuh oh-ruh*
half an hour	mitja hora	*mee-juh oh-ruh*
Monday	dilluns	*dee-lyoonz*
Tuesday	dimarts	*dee-marts*
Wednesday	dimecres	*dee-meh-kruhs*
Thursday	dijous	*dee-zhoh-oos*
Friday	divendres	*dee-ven-druhs*
Saturday	dissabte	*dee-sab-tuh*
Sunday	diumenge	*dee-oo-men-juh*

ACKNOWLEDGMENTS

The publisher would like to thank the following for their kind permission to reproduce their photographs:

Key: a-above; b-below/bottom; c-centre; f-far; l-left; r-right; t-top

123RF.com: Andrey Bayda 62cla; Alena Birukova 26tl; Mauro Celio 72cr; Iakov Filimonov 115crb; Olena Kachmar 144-5b; Pabkov 184-5t; Alena Redchenko 10ca; Marco Rubino 17t, 102-3; Zhanna Tretiakova 147br.

Alamy Stock Photo: AA World Travel Library 195clb; Michael Abid 107; age fotostock / Alfred Abad 197bl, / Gonzalo Azumendi 178b; J. Ll. Banús 82tl, / Marco Brivio 116-7t, / Rafael Campillo 148bl, / Angelo Cavalli 140-1t, / Christian Goupi 27tl, / Javier Larrea 131cb, 131crb, 152-3, 175crb, / Giuseppe Masci 120cla, / Pixtal 24crb, / Jordi Sans 132-3b, / Fco. Javier Sobrino 195tr, / Eduard Solé 148cr, / Marc Soler 96cl; ALLTRAVEL / Peter Mross 191cl, 201br; Art Collection 3 70cb; Aitor Rodero Aznarez 77cb; John Baran 191tr, 191cra,191b; Juan Bautista 133tr, 192bl; Biosphoto / Antoni Agelet 188-9b; Jordi Boixareu 13br; Xavier Calvet Camats 193t; Jordi Camí 156t, 195br; Chronicle 60-1t; Classic Image 185bl; Chris Craggs 41cl; Michele D'Ottavio 11t; Ian Dagnall 71tr; Dleiva 176-7b; domonabikeSpain 37cl; Rosmi Duaso 30-1b, 195cra; Endless Travel 169cr; eye35 stock 97tr; Christophe Faugere 196-7t; Iakov Filimonov 181bl; Aaron Fink 71cra; Peter Forsberg 91tr; Peter Forsberg / Europe 146br; Fototext 157tr; Granger Historical Picture Archive / NYC © Successió Miró / ADAGP, Paris and DACS, London 2019 129tl; hemis.fr / Lionel Montico 93br, / Ludovic Maisant 122tl; / René Mattes 75crb,/ Fundacio Joan Miro © Successió Miró / ADAGP, Paris and DACS, London 2019 128-9b; Heritage Image Partnership Ltd / Index / Mithra Index 47cl, 177tr; imageBROKER / Christian Hütter 189ftr, / Daniel Schoenen / Barcelona Pavilion architect Ludwig Mies van der Rohe © DACS 2019 135b, / Fabian von Poser 191cr; INTERFOTO / portrait of Pablo Picasso © Succession Picasso / DACS, London 2019 79clb; Invictus SARL / Citrus Stock 117bl; Juha Jarvinen 89bc; Pawel Kazmierczak 52tl; Andrey Khrobostov 106fcrb; Brian Kinney 36-7b; Jason Knott 200clb; Lanmas 59crb, 61tr, 61cla, 61br, 62clb; Chris Lawrence 101tr; Paul Lindsay 10clb; Lobro 84crb; Look / Andreas Strauss 20bl, 123br, / Juergen Richter 28-9t; Lophius 198tl; Luis Pina Photography 138-9t; Stefano Politi Markovina 41tr, 75clb, 76-7t, 77br, 113tr, 158cr, 190bl; Bob Masters 155tr; Matt May 30tl; Hercules Milas 42br, 55cla; Hugh Mitton 40-1t; J.Enrique Molina 131cra; Graham Mulrooney 140bl; Newscom / BJ Warnick 147tr; North Wind Picture Archives 58t; Matthias Oesterle 48-9b, 55crb; Photo12 / Ann Ronan Picture Library 63clb; PhotoBliss 58cb; The Picture Art Collection 61cb; Pictureproject 114-5t; Prisma Archivo 59tl, 59tr, 59cla, 60tl, 60bc, 61tl, 106cb, 131tl, 171cra, 193br; Luca Quadrio 146-7t, 186t; Campillo Rafael 20crb, 56cl; Robertharding / Neale Clark 109tc; Pere Sanz 194b; Howard Sayer 24cr; Science History Images 97br; Camila Se 109cra; Paul Shaddick 191br; M.Sobreira 11br, 53tr; Marc Soler 28bl, 88tl; Kumar Sriskandan 38-9b; Marek Stepan 10-1b, 157b; StockFood GmbH / Inga Wandinger 195crb; Stockimo / Robis 31tr;

travelstock44.de / Juergen Held 151bl; Lucas Vallecillos 22t, 34-5t, 57cl, 74clb, 74b, 75bc, 90-1b, 96t, 121bl, 158-9b, 177cra, 184bl, 186cra; VSL / McPHOTO / blickwinkel 8cla; Ken Welsh 99tl; Andrew Wilson 161tr; Jan Wlodarczyk 71tc, 85clb, 98bl; World History Archive 171tl; World History Archive / AG 106clb; Gregory Wrona 41crb, 81crb; Chun Ju Wu 111b; Xavier Fores - Joana Roncero 81b; Xinhua 13cr; ZUMA Press; Inc. / SOPA Images / Ramon Costa 57clb.

AWL Images: Hemis 82-3b; Tom Mackie 187br; Stefano Politi Markovina 42tr; Travel Pix Collection 113tl.

Bridgeman Images: Museu Picasso, Barcelona / Las Meninas (3rd October 1957) by Pablo Picasso © Succession Picasso / DACS, London 2019 79bl.

El Brogit – www.elbrogit.com: 39br.

Used with permission of Casa Batlló (www.casabatllo.es): 37, 84, 112-3 all.

Centre de Cultura Contemporània de Barcelona – CCCB: Miquel Tavern 34bl.

Collage Art & Cocktails Social Club: 49br.

Compartir: Francesc Guillamet 12clb, 31cl.

Depositphotos Inc: Alexsalcedo 12t; boule1301 32tl; kovgabor79 43br; Sanguer 46-7b.

Dorling Kindersley: Max Alexander 169br.

Dreamstime.com: 22tomtom 62tl; Claudiu Alexandru 112bl; Steve Allen 171cr; Aprescindere 29bl; Sergio Torres Baus 100bl; Daniel Sanchez Blasco 27cla; Blitzkoenig 18tl, 124-5; Artur Bogacki 47tr; Boule13 154-5b; Brasilnut 52-3b; Citalliance 33t; Juan Bautista Cofreces 54-5t; Cristian64 179br; Danflcreativo 76bl; Dinogeromella 26tr; Ego450 145ca; Elxeneize 94-5; Maria Luisa Lopez Estivill 40-1b; Iakov Filimonov 33clb, 56cra, 120t, 139bl; Veronika Galkina 174-5t; Gelia 191crb; Gerold Grotelueschen 44tr; Henrikhl 179bl; Juan Polo Ignacio 44bl; Ivana Jankovic 189tr; Jarcosa 56crb; García Juan 70crb; Veniamin Kraskov 145cla; Sebastian Kummer 175br; Bogdan Lazar 80t; Marcopachiega 57crb; Marcorubino 8-9b, 37crb, 47br, 110t, 134tl; Alberto Masnovo 129cra; Mavrinvlad 22tr; Jelena Maximova 22cl; Juan Moyano 31br, 43tr; Roland Nagy 85tr; Natursports 51br; Olgacov 172t; Clement Mantion Pierre Olivier 35b; Photoprofi30 27tr; Radub85 64-5; Robert309 163; Mauro Rodrigues 189cr; Arseniy Rogov 20t; Tiberiu Sahlean 179bc; Schlenger86 43cla; Seadam 51cla; Olena Serditova 118-9b; Jacek Sopotnicki 88-9t; Tanaonte 54-5b; Tomas1111 2-3; 46tr; 85br; Toniflap 20cr; Pavlo Vakhrushev 110c; Alvaro German Vilela 53cl; Vitalyedush 113cra; Xantana 11cr; Tetiana Zbrodko 169t; Мария Канатова 4.

Elsa Y Fred: 26cla.

© Escudería Targa Iberia: 50-1t.

© FC BARCELONA: 147clb.

Main Contributors Sally Davies, Ben Ffrancon Davies, Mary-Ann Gallagher, Roger Williams

Additional Contributors Mary Jane Aladren, Pepita Arias, Emma Dent Coad, Rebecca Doulton, Josefina Fernandez, Nick Rider, David Stone, Judy Thomson, Clara Villanueva, Suzanne Wales

Senior Editor Ankita Awasthi Tröger

Senior Designer Tania Da Silva Gomes

Project Editors Emma Grundy Haigh, Brana Vladisavljevic

Project Art Editor Dan Bailey

Designers Hansa Babra, Kitty Glavin, Jordan Lambley, Priyanka Thakur, Vinita Venugopal

Factchecker Suzanne Wales

Editors Rachel Thompson, Lucy Sara-Kelly

Proofreader Sarah MacLeod

Indexer Hilary Bird

Senior Picture Researcher Ellen Root

Picture Research Marta Bescos, Manpreet Kaur, Sumita Khatwani, Vagisha Pushp, Rituraj Singh

Illustrators Stephen Conlin, Isidoro González-Adalid Cabezas (Acanto Arquitectura y Urbanismo S.L.), Claire Littlejohn, Maltings Partnership, John Woodcock

Cartographic Editor James Macdonald

Cartography Zafar ul-Islam Khan, Animesh Pathak

Jacket Designers Dan Bailey, Maxine Pedliham

Jacket Picture Research Susie Watters

Senior DTP Designer Jason Little

DTP George Nimmo

Producer Kariss Ainsworth

Managing Editor Hollie Teague

Art Director Maxine Pedliham

Publishing Director Georgina Dee

First edition 1999

Published in Great Britain by Dorling Kindersley Limited, 80 Strand, London, WC2R 0RL

Published in the United States by DK Publishing, 1450 Broadway, Suite 801, New York, NY 10018

Copyright © 1999, 2020 Dorling Kindersley Limited
A Penguin Random House Company
19 20 21 22 10 9 8 7 6 5 4 3 2 1

A CIP catalog record for this book is available from the British Library.

A catalog record for this book is available from the Library of Congress.

ISSN: 1542 1554
ISBN: 978 0 2414 0795 0

Printed and bound in China.

www.dk.com

MIX
Paper from
responsible sources
FSC™ C018179
www.fsc.org

The information in this DK Eyewitness Travel Guide is checked regularly.
Every effort has been made to ensure that this book is as up-to-date as possible at the time of going to press. Some details, however, such as telephone numbers, opening hours, prices, gallery hanging arrangements and travel information, are liable to change. The publishers cannot accept responsibility for any consequences arising from the use of this book, nor for any material on third party websites, and cannot guarantee that any website address in this book will be a suitable source of travel information. We value the views and suggestions of our readers very highly. Please write to: Publisher, DK Eyewitness Travel Guides, Dorling Kindersley, 80 Strand, London, WC2R 0RL, UK, or email: travelguides@dk.com